Religious Faith
and Twentieth-Century Man

Religious Faith
and Twentieth-Century Man

F. C. HAPPOLD

CROSSROAD · NEW YORK

1981
The Crossroad Publishing Company
18 East 41st Street, New York, NY 10017

Printed in the United States of America

Library of Congress Cataloging in Publication Data

Happold, Frederick Crossfield, 1893-
Religious faith and twentieth-century man.

Bibliography: p.
Includes index.
1. Christianity—20th century. 2. Mysticism.
I. Title.
BR121.2.H33   1981   230   81-518
ISBN 0-8245-0046-6   AACR1

Contents

To HERBERT BUTTERFIELD in appreciation of a long and valued friendship I dedicate this book

Foreword

The title of this book sets side by side two realities that seem to have lost touch with one another—religious faith on the one hand, twentieth-century man on the other. For surely twentieth-century man is typically the secularized man, the man who in an age of science and high technology has discarded religion and may even think that he has outgrown it. Yet emancipation from religion does not seem to have brought us the freedom and happiness that the nineteenth-century critics of religion expected. We are today more bewildered than ever, subject to many anxieties, cut off from our spiritual heritage and afflicted with the rootlessness which that implies. Feuerbach believed that religion alienates man from his true being, but the decline of religion since his time has been accompanied by a growing sense of alienation deeper than any known before.

Few persons have been more sensitive to the contradictions of our time than was Dr F. C. Happold, and his book remains one of the best guides I know for those who are seeking a new wholeness. It is one of those rare works which succeeds in being non-technical while addressing itself to the most difficult problems and drawing on an amazingly wide range of knowledge—scientific and philosophical, religious and secular, spiritual and psychological, modern and traditional. On the whole, this is a hopeful and encouraging book. The author believes that while we are indeed passing through a dark night, when the foundations on which the Western world relied for so many centuries seem to have crumbled, nevertheless it is a time of transition. If old beliefs have lost their credibility, there is on the other hand, he believes, a new awakening and an expansion of consciousness and perception. We have to become alive to it.

'Living on the intersection' is how Dr Happold describes his own engagement in the modern world, and it is this attitude that he also commends to his readers. The person who lives on the intersection refuses to let his life be diminished or truncated or even crippled by allowing some of its dimensions to be lopped off. He strives to keep himself open to the currents of thought and movements of spirit that converge upon him from different directions. Of course, he does this not uncritically, but seeks to build a coherent synthesis out of the contributions that are brought to him. Thus, to give a few examples, he seeks to reconcile scientific knowledge of the universe with the insights of religion, the findings of modern psychology with the spiritual wisdom of the past, his own specific tradition (be it Christian or Jewish or Buddhist or humanist) with other traditions which he meets in our pluralist world, the claims of contemplation with those of action, his individual integrity with the need to participate in and learn from society, and so on.

It may seem an ambitious ideal. Certainly it is a vision of human life which, in its fulness and richness, far surpasses the stunted, limited, superficial ways in which so many pass their lives in the contemporary world. But it is not an impossible ideal. It is one which the author himself found satisfying, to such an extent that he felt impelled to commend it to others in this book. One should add that it is an ideal with considerable openness of texture. What Dr Happold sets forth is a comprehensive pattern, the details of which each individual will need to decide for himself in accordance with his peculiar gifts and needs.

Fundamental to Dr Happold's pattern for living is a vein of mysticism. Let the reader not be frightened off by this. It is not easy to say just what mysticism is. Perhaps what is essential to it is a deep feeling of reverence and kinship for the reality that meets us in the environing world, including the worlds both of nature and of persons. Few of us indeed would hope or expect to share the vision of the great contemplatives who have appeared in all the major religious traditions—men and women of profound spiritual sensitivity who seem to have established an intimate *rapport* with the very heart of reality. Yet, through reading their works and sharing their thoughts, it is possible for all of us to gain some understanding of the experience that was theirs, and to have some participation in it.

But if the mystic has a vision of the deepest reality, he is very cautious in what he says about it. As likely as not, he will say that it is indescribable, ineffable, inexpressible. Perhaps, in Wittgenstein's language, the mystical 'shows' itself, but it cannot be encompassed by speech. On the other hand, it can be hinted at through symbols and metaphors, myth and poetry, ways of using language which are different from everyday literal descriptions, but which nevertheless open our eyes to realities we would otherwise have missed, so that this whole realm of mystical insight can rightly be called cognitive. Mysticism affords a vision of the unity that underlies all the multitudinous phenomena of life and all the varied events of history— the unity that we call the One, the Holy, the Absolute, even God.

Dr Happold believes that 'the only possible religion for twentieth-century man is a mystical religion, and all theological language must be recognized as a language of symbols'. Those for whom conventional religion with its definite dogmas and its popularly understood idea of God as a kind of celestial monarch have become incredible are invited to find a renewal of faith in the mystical approach

7

to God. Dr Happold has obvious sympathies with such modern theologians as Paul Tillich, John Robinson and others who have criticized the traditional Judeo-Christian understanding of God and have stressed much more the immanence of the divine in the natural order and the closeness of God to the world. Of course, there is nothing new in all this—it links up directly with the centuries-old tradition of mysticism, as we find it not only among the Christian mystics of Europe, such as John Eckhart and Nicholas of Cusa, but among mystics in other religions.

Dr Happold himself was something of a mystic. He tells us in this book about some of his own mystical experiences, so it is not some second-hand faith that he is commending, but one rooted in his own experience—so vivid and so deeply rooted that for him there can be no doubting of its validity. But he is not trying to impose on us his own individualistic preference. He links up his own experience with the whole mystical tradition, with the literature of which he is thoroughly acquainted. When we consider this tradition, we see also its relevance for our time and why it has appealed to Dr Happold and other twentieth-century persons. In venturing to speak of the Holy or God, mysticism does supply that lost dimension in the experience of a secular age; but in speaking of the Holy or God in a modest, undogmatic way, frankly recognizing the ineffability of the Holy and the inadequacy of our highest symbols, mysticism chimes in with the cautious mood of modern philosophy.

Here we must touch more directly on the relation of mystical religion to contemporary science. Just as the mystic acknowledges the inadequate and therefore metaphorical nature of his language about God, so physics after Einstein and Planck has come to acknowledge the symbolic character of its language. While that language articulates an understanding of the physical world, it does not claim to give a literal description. In this regard, the twentieth-century scientific picture is far more open to the possibility of a religious interpretation of the universe than was the nineteenth-century picture, with its hard solid atoms performing an eternal ballet according to the eternal iron laws of mechanics. We are confronted today with a universe which has an openness and a mystery by no means incompatible with the mystical vision. Indeed, according to Dr Happold, 'that vision, far from being imposed on something alien, arises out of the very texture of the cosmos as we are now beginning to see it'. He was especially struck by the fact that both mystics and physicists are driven to the paradoxical use of language. That is to say, to account for the complexity of what confronts them, they are driven to make apparently contradictory statements about it, and yet to maintain that both sides of the contradiction are true. This is what Nicholas of Cusa called the *coincidentia oppositorum*, the coming together of contraries.

Still another dimension of the 'intersection' described by Dr Happold is opened up by the work of psychologists on the role of the unconscious and the part played by symbols that arise out of those depths of the mind. In particular, it was the work of C. G. Jung that seemed to offer a bridge between religion and modern research into the mind.

How, it may be asked, do the views set forth in this book stand in relation to orthodox Christianity? A glance at the chapter 'The Splendour of the Christ' will make it clear that we are not being offered a new religion, nor is Dr Happold suggesting a merging of all the religions into some featureless syncretism. His hope is that existing faiths will be quickened and renewed through the deepening of their mystical insights and through a better understanding of what they are trying to say. This will not destroy the great religious traditions, though it will lead to a re-thinking of their credal expressions and will also lead to a better understanding among them.

This book has much to contribute toward promoting spiritual integrity in our time.

JOHN MACQUARRIE

Christ Church
Oxford

Introduction

THERE is more than one way of writing a book of this sort. The author can strive to be coolly impersonal and objective, keeping himself entirely in the background and, though his book cannot but be in some way an expression of himself and his experiences, the reader will be unable to form any picture of him, nor will he have any knowledge of the experience out of which the book grew. Some would say that that is the proper way to write a book of this sort.

It is not the way, however, that I intend to write it. Recently I read a review by Philip Toynbee which contained these sentences:

> I begin to suspect that all present attempts at majestic general statements, all forms of polymath eclecticism, all Religions for Modern Man and Free Men's Worships are as useless in our time as are all attempts to restore or modernise traditional religious beliefs ... All these liberal-minded 'syntheses' by psychologically inclined churchmen and christianising Marxists, by biologists who listen to Bach and novelists who understand the second law of thermodynamics, by mystical astronomers and humane Catholics – they all, it seems to me, seep into the sludge of a common delta where mud, sea and sky (however blue) are lost in a universal grey opacity.
>
> And the answer? Simply to wait – on God or whatever it may be, and in the meantime to leave the general alone and to concentrate all our natural energies and curiosities on the specific, the idiosyncratic, the personal. ...

In part at least Philip Toynbee is right. We do not know enough. We cannot do otherwise than wait – in contemplation, in meditation, in prayer, prayer in its fullest sense, which goes far beyond petitionary prayer. But surely, side by side with that, there is the call to think, to analyse, to try to understand. For the intelligent to avoid that call is in-

deed a *trahison des clercs*. 'There must be a creed, a fundamental statement.' The puzzled young people in Wells's
novel speak for our age. Or at least there must be some
attempt at framing a working hypothesis; for, as one of the
characters in a book by Aldous Huxley put it: 'No working
hypothesis means no motive for starting the research, no
reason for making one experiment rather than another, no
rational theory for bringing sense or order to the observed
facts.'*

So, let this book be read, not as an attempt at a majestic
general statement, but as a humble, rather fumbling attempt
to find a working hypothesis, an attempt made by one
particular twentieth-century man who has tried to throw his
mind open to the impact of the thought of his age, who has
during a long lifetime undergone certain experiences, which
have been to him significant and meaningful, and which
have determined the pattern of his thought and belief, his
world-view, at the particular moment he is writing this
book. 'Made by one particular twentieth-century man':
therefore any working hypothesis which is reached will be,
perforce, personal, the outcome of personal experience. A
great part of the book will be description and analysis: it
will be, to that extent, impersonal, general and abstract. To
the extent, however, that it is selection and interpretation,
I would wish it to be considered as personal, idiosyncratic,
the fruit of one man's experience. So it ought, perhaps, to
begin with autobiography.

Valuable as a chapter of autobiography can be in enabling
the reader to understand the author's thought – the chapter
'Personalia' in Huxley's *Religion without Revelation* adds
much to one's appreciation of Huxley's position – I do not
intend to burden him with the story of my life. There were,
however, two experiences which happened to me while I
was an undergraduate at Cambridge between 1912 and 1914

* Huxley: *Time Must Have a Stop* (Chatto & Windus).

which I regard as among the most vital and significant of my life. To tell of them will, I believe, be conducive to a better understanding of my book. Had I not known these experiences not only my spiritual development but also the whole pattern of my thought would have been different. At the time I knew nothing about mysticism; I do not think I was even familiar with the word. My later studies in mysticism have, however, enabled me to recognize them as in a true sense mystical. I will describe them in the words I used in my own 'case history', which I included, with some dozen others, in the first section, entitled 'The Timeless Moment', in the Anthology of my book, *Mysticism: a Study and an Anthology*.

It happened in my room in Peterhouse in the evening of 1 February 1913, when I was an undergraduate at Cambridge. If I say that Christ came to me I should be using conventional words which would carry no precise meaning; for Christ comes to men and women in different ways. When I tried to record the experience at the time I used the imagery of the vision of the Holy Grail; it seemed to me to be like that. There was, however, no sensible vision. There was just the room, with its shabby furniture and the fire burning in the grate and the red shaded lamp on the table. But the room was filled by a Presence, which in a strange way was both about me and within me, like light or warmth. I was overwhelmingly possessed by Someone who was not myself, and yet I felt I was more myself than I had ever been before. I was filled with an intense happiness, an almost unbearable joy, such as I had never known before and have never known since. And over all was a deep sense of peace and security and certainty. Some experiences of this sort, which I have found recorded, lasted a very short time. Mine lasted several hours. What time I went to bed I do not know, but when I awoke in the morning it was still there. During the day it faded. It was very wonderful and quite unforgettable. . . .

The other experience of which I must tell happened a little

later in the same room. I have always thought of it as a continuation and completion of that I have described; it 'felt' the same. This time, however, it seemed that a voice was speaking to me. It was not sensibly audible; it spoke within me. The words were strange: 'Those who sought the city found the wood; and those who sought the wood found the city.' Put into cold print they sound nonsensical. Yet I felt vividly that they meant something very important, that they were the key to a secret.

What did they mean? What is their significance in relation to the key-ideas of this book?

'The room was filled by a Presence, which in a strange way was both about me and within me, like light or warmth.'

I do not think that I could ever question the existence of God for, though I do not deceive myself by thinking that I can apprehend God intellectually, I have 'met' God. My position must always remain that of St Paul in the poem of that name by F. W. H. Myers:

> Whoso has felt the spirit of the Highest
> Cannot confound or doubt Him nor deny.
> Yea with one voice, O world, though thou deniest,
> Stand thou on that side, for on this am I.

'The words were strange: "Those who sought the city found the wood; and those who sought the wood found the city." Put into cold print they sound nonsensical. Yet I felt vividly that they meant something very important, that they were the key to a secret.'

How important a key it was I was not to discover until many years later. I know now that this experience was an intellectual mystical vision of the most profound significance. It has taken a lifetime to realize it in its fullness. It will be necessary to say a good deal about it later.

Another experience, to me of similar significance, happened much later, on the evening of 18 April 1936, the evening before my son was born. I will give it in the words used in the 'case-history' mentioned above:

It happened to me on the evening of 18 April 1936, the evening of the day before my son was born. My first child had been still-born, and, as I lay in bed, I was very anxious about my wife and much disturbed in mind. And then a great peace came over me. I was conscious of a lovely, unexplainable pattern in the texture of things, a pattern of which everyone and everything was a part; and weaving the pattern was a Power; and that Power was what we faintly call Love. I realized that we are not lonely atoms in a cold, unfriendly, indifferent universe, but that each of us is linked up in a rhythm, of which we may be unconscious, and which we can never really know, but to which we can submit ourselves trustfully and unreservedly.

Many others have had a similar vision. Like myself they understand what Bernard Bosanquet meant when, of salvation, he wrote:

And now we are saved absolutely, we need not say from what, we are at home in the universe, and in principle and in the main, feeble and timid creatures as we are, there is nothing anywhere in the world or without it that can make us afraid.*

True, there is something in men which compels them to rebel against an irrational universe and which will not allow them to conceive of the Divine Being except as One who is the sum total, and much more, of everything that they, in their highest moments, feel to be most beautiful and good and true. Nevertheless, though God as Love can be realized as inner experience, it cannot be rationally demonstrated and there is much in the world which seems to contradict it.

Three things ought to be said at this point to avoid misunderstanding. First, in recording these personal experiences I would wish to guard against giving the impress-

* Bosanquet: *What Religion Is* (Macmillan).

ion that I am more spiritually endowed than I really am. The significant thing is that they should have happened to one such as I know myself to be.

Secondly mystical experience has no validity except for the one who experiences it; it does not constitute proof for anyone else. What can be said, however, is that when an examination of the totality of mystical experience, that is of mystical experience as it is found throughout man's history, among people of different religions and philosophical beliefs, of different geographical and cultural environments, and at different levels of spiritual development, reveals common characteristics, then it becomes a body of evidence which must be taken into consideration in the exploration of the nature of the Real.

And finally, the contact with That which we call God found in mystical experience does not entitle one to make a metaphysical statement about the nature of God. Of God as He is in Himself, nothing can be said; He simply *is*. 'Who says that Spirit is not known, knows; who claims that he knows, knows nothing. The ignorant think that Spirit lies within knowledge, the wise man knows it beyond knowledge. Spirit is known through revelation.' So speaks the Kena-Upanishad. Communion with God may and usually does take a personal form; He is experienced as *a person*. That does not entitle one to describe God as personal, for what is being described is not God as He is Himself, but the nature of His self-giving, i.e. God-for-me.

The theme of this book is the spiritual crisis of our age; it is an inquiry into the nature of the religious consciousness of twentieth-century man. To enter on a study of the operation of religious consciousness is to carry out a piece of research in the science of the non-rational. For the things with which religion deals cannot be reduced to the rational without losing most of their meaning and significance. That is not to say that religion is *ir*rational. It is to say that there is a realm of experience which cannot be adequately probed by or explained in terms of the intellect. It is the realm of *the mystical*.

The theme of *the mystical* runs through this book, which might almost be given the sub-title, 'An Essay in the Mystical'. What is here meant by the mystical? Much will be written later; but let us here try to get a general idea of how the term is going to be interpreted.

'Not *how* the world is, is the mystical, but *that* it is.' That cryptic phrase of Ludwig Wittgenstein, which will be further considered later, though it does not cover everything that is meant, carries us some way. It is more subtly described by the Zen Buddhist, Hsuan-chiao:

You cannot take hold of it, nor can you get rid of it;
While you can do neither, it goes on its own way;
You remain silent and it speaks; you speak and it is silent:
The great gate of charity is wide open with no obstruction
    whatever before it.*

Yet the mystical is *real*. It can be *felt*. Though it can neither be described adequately in rational categories nor spoken about 'meaningfully', it can, in a real sense, be *known*. It is the *inexpressible*. 'There is indeed the inexpressible,' wrote Wittgenstein, 'it *shows* itself; it is the mystical.'

And at the heart of the mystical is the That which has no name, but which is called by a hundred names; which has no form but which is manifested in a thousand forms, God, the Ultimate Reality, of Whom, or Which, the anonymous author of *The Cloud of Unknowing* wrote:

Of all creatures and their works, yea, of the works of God's self, may a man through grace have fullness of knowing, and well he can think of them; but of God Himself can no man think.

All this is true. Yet provided the nature of religious experience is clearly realized and the limitations inherent in

* Quoted in Watts: *Behold the Spirit* (John Murray).

any examination of it accepted, it is possible to examine man's religious experience rationally in the same way that it is possible to examine rationally any other aspect of experience, and to describe, analyse and interpret it in rational terms. One may consider it as an element in evolutionary and historical development; one may analyse it in psychological terms; one may survey it in relation to other types of experience. All such descriptions, analyses and interpretations are valuable and illuminating, even though one is always forced to acknowledge a 'more', a point at which intellect falls back, beyond which nothing rationally meaningful can be said and the only language is the language of symbol.

Something is happening in the world. We are conscious of it all around us. Our era is said to be the era of the emergence of 'secular man', man who has 'come of age', and has no longer any need of 'God'. This may be true; but may it not also be the era of the emergence of a new sort of spiritual man? I would ask you to consider this possibility. May it not be that we are in the midst of – or should one say on the verge of? – one of those mental and spiritual 'leaps', those 'disclosure situations' (to use a current phrase), which have happened before in the history of mankind, eras when the corporate mentality and spirituality of man shift and expand and new vistas and interpretations of the universe open up?

As one ponders and tries to understand the present situation of the world, thoughts hover on the brink of illumination, and then become obscure; as one tries to describe, analyse and interpret it, words break. Ideas which represent a new advance in human thought and awareness come in wordless form, as dim intuitions, faint anticipations and formless gropings. Only later do they become clear and a language is evolved capable of expressing them. If at times this book is uncertain and contradictory, if sometimes ideas are lacking in clarity and precision, it is almost inevitable that it should be so.

The first task is an obvious one. It is to survey the spiritual crisis of twentieth-century man and to try to disentangle the chief elements in it. Let us start with that.

I

The Spiritual Crisis of Twentieth-Century Man

'AT the back of all there surely has to be a creed, a fundamental statement, put in language which does not conflict with every reality we know about the world. We don't want to be put off with serpents and fig-leaves and sacrificial lambs. We want a creed in modern English, sir. And we can't find it.'

So spoke one of the puzzled young people in a conversation with the country vicar in H. G. Wells's novel, *The Babes in the Darkling Wood*. It is a vivid, if not very profound, expression of the spiritual crisis of twentieth-century man.

To say that the world is at one of those crisis-points in its history when an old order is breaking up and a new order coming to birth, is a platitude. Everyone is to a greater or lesser degree conscious of it. There have been so many attempted analyses of its nature that one has grown weary of them. Analyses made by those who are involved in such a crisis are never complete and often incorrect. The twelfth-century Bernard of Cluny wrote early in the century a hymn which began:

> The world is very evil;
> The times are waxing late;
> Be sober and keep vigil,
> The Judge is at the gate.

Yet that century saw not only a great flowering in the cultural life of Western Europe – it was the century of the rise of towns, of the beginnings of Gothic architecture, of the emergence of vernacular literature, of the revival of Latin studies and the founding of the first European universities, and, through contacts with the Moslem world, of the re-discovery of Greek science – but also the revival of spiritual and mystical life.

Nevertheless, incomplete and tentative though the analysis may be, one is compelled to try to analyse and assess. Only thus is it possible to reach some sort of working hypothesis as a guide to thought and action.

The spiritual crisis of modern man is bound up with and is the result of two of the most far-reaching developments in the history of mankind.

The first of these is the elimination of distance. Vastly improved communications have unified our globe. Inter-continental telephone, wireless, sound radio and television have linked up thought and speech. There is now only one world, of which each of us is a part; with a consequent change for good or evil in our attitudes and thought-patterns. This change is expressed very vividly in Martin Skinner's satirical poem, *Letters to Malaya**:

> Gone are the days when madness was confined
> By seas and hills from spreading through mankind;
> When though a Nero fooled upon a string,
> Wisdom still reigned unruffled in Pekin;
> And God in welcome smiled from Buddha's face,
> Though Calvin in Geneva preached of grace.
> For now our linked-up globe has shrunk so small,
> One Hitler on it means mad days for all.

The second is the result of the discoveries of the scientists. Aptly does Arnold Toynbee, in his *Study of History*, speak of a 'new dimension of the spiritual universe brought to light by the psychologists' and a 'new dimension of the physical universe brought to light by the atomic physicists'. To these must be added recent discoveries in the domain of astronomy, which have revealed a stellar universe so in-

* Published by Putnam.

credibly vast that human thought falls back in its attempt to comprehend it.

It is possible to trace the beginnings of these transformations as far back as the publication of Dalton's atomic theory in 1800, or even to the Scientific Revolution of the seventeenth century. The discoveries which have more than any others revolutionized the thought of twentieth-century man belong, however, to our own century. Rutherford's earliest work on atomic physics was not done until after 1900. The work of Freud did not begin to attract wide attention, at any rate in this country, until after the First World War. The most startling discoveries in astronomy are later still.

A new picture of the physical universe and of the place of this planet and of man in it, a new picture of the inner urges which control and direct men's thought, feeling and action, have emerged. And, as these new pictures have more and more permeated the corporate mentality, the pattern of man's thinking has changed. Even among those on whom the intellectual impact is slight, there is a psychological impact, which few escape.

In the beginning God created the heaven and the earth. And the earth was waste and void; and darkness was upon the face of the deep: and the spirit of God moved upon the face of the waters.

And God said, Let there be light: and there was light . . .

And God created man in his own image, in the image of God created he him.

So runs the splendid opening of the Book of Genesis. The last sentence has been parodied 'Man creates God in his own image.' The parody contains an element of truth. The majority of men are not highly spiritually gifted nor are many equipped with minds of a philosophical bent. They are obliged to proceed from the known to the unknown. The *That* which *is*, is unknown and unknowable by the human intellect. If it were not so It would not be God. At the intellectual level men are thus inevitably forced to make 'images' of the Ineffable and Ungraspable; and these images are influenced by and bound up with their picture of the nature of the universe and of themselves. The history of the search by man for a fuller knowledge of God is littered with discarded images of Him.

Consider the intellectual, and even more the psychological, effects of the latest statements of the astronomers on the extent of the universe. We are told that the light-waves from the cluster of galaxies in Hydra which reach us have travelled through space for two thousand million light years. This cluster of galaxies is only one of numerous galaxies, each one made up of millions of stars, separated from each other by immeasurable stretches of intergalactic space. Our own solar system is a minute part of the Milky Way, which is made up of some ten million stars.

Ponder this picture of the universe and then put to yourself the question: What is God? What am I and what is my relation to the immensity of the That which I name God? Men can no longer rest in an image of God which appeared reasonable in the light of earlier cosmologies.

The nature of the spiritual crisis of our time has seldom been better expressed than by Father Pierre Teilhard de Chardin in the introduction to his *Le Milieu Divin*,* where he writes:

The enrichment and ferment of religious thought in our time has undoubtedly been caused by the revelation of the size and unity of the world all around us and within us. All around us the physical sciences are endlessly extending the abysses of time and space, and ceaselessly discerning new relationships between the elements of the universe. Within us a whole world of affinities and interrelated sympathies, as old as the human soul, is being awakened by the stimulus of these great discoveries, and what has hitherto been dreamed

* Published by Collins and Harper & Row Inc.

rather than experienced is at last taking shape and consistency. Scholarly and discriminating among serious thinkers, simple or didactic among the half-educated, the aspirations towards a vaster and more organic *one*, and the premonitions of unknown forces and their application in new fields, are the same, and are emerging simultaneously on all sides.

And he poses the question:

Is the Christ of the Gospels, imagined and loved within the dimensions of a Mediterranean world, capable of still embracing and still forming the centre of our prodigiously expanding universe? Is the world not in the process of becoming more vast, more close, more dazzling than Jehovah? Will it not burst our religion asunder? Eclipse our God?

The publication of Darwin's *The Origin of Species*, in 1859, and of Lyell's *The Antiquity of Man*, in 1863, had demonstrated not only that this earth was immensely older than it had been thought to be, but also that it had not come into existence in its present form, but was the product of age-long evolution and change. Christians of the nineteenth century were called upon painfully to adjust their view of the nature of the inspiration of the Bible to this new knowledge. By the end of the century the new knowledge had, however, been gradually accepted and assimilated by Christian thinkers.

During our own century a new challenge to religious conceptions has been presented by the depth psychologists. The clinical work of the Viennese psychologist, Sigmund Freud, at the beginning of the century led him to put forward a new system and explanation of the nature and workings of our subjective feelings. The practical importance of the work of Freud and his successors was that it made possible much more enlightened methods of dealing with all sorts of psychological disorders and maladjustments. Freud's discoveries, however, raised important philosophical and theological issues. If his account of how our thoughts, emotions and feelings work is correct, what shall we say of our sense of the divine, of all those beliefs, aspirations and emotions with which religion deals. Freud's interpretation of his own findings was anti-religious. He explained the religious urge in man as an illusory rationalization of unconscious wishes, as a projection to compensate for an infantile sense of helplessness. God was a projection of the father-image, a fantasy substitute for an actual and not altogether satisfactory father. For him sexuality – he uses the term in a special sense – centred in the incest-wish, was the dominant psychological factor, and this inherent sexuality explained man's desire for union with God.

There are other possible theories, as Jung has demonstrated in his numerous writings.* Nevertheless, the vastly enlarged knowledge of the inner operations of the psyche gave a new picture of the inherent religious urge in man which can be very disturbing and result in complete scepticism, but which can also be illuminating and exciting and lead to a richer and fuller faith.

That many are conscious of the challenge which new knowledge has presented to religious faith was evident when, in 1963, the Bishop of Woolwich wrote an article in the *Observer*, with the title, 'Our Image of God must go', followed two days later by the publication of his book, *Honest to God*. In his article and book the Bishop said nothing very new, and some thought he did not say it very well. He was merely putting forward views which some theologians had already expressed in their writings for a considerable time. The general public seldom, however, reads the books written by theologians; a great many, however, read the *Observer* and, as a result of the article, many read the book. Seldom has an article in the press and a little paperback aroused so great interest and discussion.

* See below pp. 64–9.

The Bishop found himself a national figure. The issues he had raised were the subject of discussions on radio and television, of articles in every sort of newspaper, of a deluge of letters to the Press and of sermons in the churches. Two weeks after the appearance of the Bishop of Woolwich's article the *Observer* printed an article by Sir Julian Huxley with the title 'Religion without God', which ended with a plea for 'a number of participants to take part in the great discussion and join in the search for the larger truth and more fruitful pattern of belief which are waiting to be elicited.'

Even when allowances are made for that element of sensationalism which is characteristic of a great deal of the Press, it was clear that, in spite of a growing secularism, a deep and widespread interest in religion still exists, but that the ways in which religious faith and belief are often expressed have little meaning or effect. A better title for the Bishop's article would have been 'Our image of God *has gone*'. That is certainly true for many, if not for all.

If one considers the present situation from the point of view of Christianity, it seems to be as follows: Christianity now faces a crisis not dissimilar to that which it was called upon to face in its beginnings. Jesus was at first thought of merely as the Messiah for whom the Jews had long waited. His revelation was to the Jews alone and had no concern with the non-Jewish world. The New Testament tells how, not without opposition, that conception changed. The revelation was seen as a revelation not to the Jews alone, but to the whole world. The mission of Christianity was to be a universal religion.

How would the early Christian, such as St Paul, interpret the word, universal? Their 'world' was the Mediterranean world, the lands surrounding the Mediterranean Sea, which had been welded together into a political whole by the Roman conquests. In order to become a universal religion for its own world Christianity had to make its peace with and take into itself the thought-patterns, spiritual and conceptual, of that world, *and that without losing its essential revelation.* The words in italics are important. Now Christianity is called upon to face up to, not the limited world of the Mediterranean, but the whole globe, with its other higher religions, some of them more spiritually aware and more redolent of the divine compassion than conventional Christianity has sometimes been. Not only that, it is also called upon to face up to those new dimensions of the physical universe revealed by the astronomers and quantum physicists and of the new dimension of the spiritual universe revealed by the psychologists. To this must be added the challenge of current philosophy, with its preoccupation with linguistic analysis, which demands a careful examination of every word and concept used.

In different ways and in different degrees the other higher religions, Hinduism, Buddhism, Mohammedanism, are called upon to meet similar challenges. Neither they nor Christianity can escape the impact not only of the linking up of the globe and the transformation of the scientific and historical world-views, but also, and perhaps most important, the fact that the thought and feelings of men have become more and more secularized. In the minds of many the image of God has faded out. Modern man, it is said, has opted for a secular world; he has come of age; he has no longer any need of religion. Freud was in part right when he called religion a projection. It is a projection which twentieth-century man is out-growing. He may not have become better – there is too much in the modern world which prevents one from having much belief in the natural goodness of man – he feels, however, no longer the need of a God, either in the way a child feels the need of the care and protection of his parents, or as an explanation of the universe. Nor does he any longer feel the need of 'pie in the sky' to compensate him for the wretchedness of his earthly lot. For though there is still much wretchedness in the world and in parts of it there are many who still live on the verge of starvation, over large areas of the globe the material lot of men has vastly improved. We live in the era of the emergence of the Welfare State.

It is too early yet to estimate the significance of the non-religious man. If one surveys the part secularism and humanism have played since the Renaissance, one cannot but feel that it has been a beneficent one. It has been, not the Christian Church, but the scientists and humanists who have led the advance in the march towards toleration and free inquiry and towards social justice and a better life for the common man. In spite of its saints, mystics, and martyrs, the history of the Christian Church is a sorry one. It is far too much the story of intolerance, persecution and bigotry, of inquisitions, torture and burnings, of 'images' of God which had little resemblance to the loving Father or our Lord Jesus Christ, or to the inner Christ of St Paul. One can sympathize with the couplet in Martin Skinner's satirical poem, quoted above:

> And God in welcome smiled from Buddha's face,
> Though Calvin in Geneva preached of grace.

Consider the two centuries which followed the collapse of the unity of Western Christendom at the time of the Protestant Reformation. Not only did Catholics persecute Protestants and Protestants persecute Catholics, but also the dominant elements in the Protestant states persecuted their own dissenters. Some sixteenth-century German Protestant dissenters fled from Christian Germany to Mohammedan Hungary to escape persecution by their co-religionists; for there was more toleration to be found in the Ottoman than in the Holy Roman Empire. The sixteenth and seventeenth centuries were filled in Europe with religious wars. The most terrible was the Thirty Years War in Germany, from which it took Germany a century to recover. It might have ended earlier had not the Catholic Cardinal, Richelieu, utilized it in the interests of the political ambitions of France. Is it surprising that at the end of the seventeenth century men, impressed by the cool objectivity of the Scientific Revolution and tired of religious strife, cried: 'A plague on all your houses', and that the eighteenth century, the Age of Reason and the Enlightenment, was one of scepticism and a decline of spirituality?

The Hegelian interpretation of history as a perpetual conflict between thesis and antithesis, resulting in a synthesis, which becomes the thesis of the next stage, only to be met, however, by a new antithesis, is, if not pressed too far, a tenable interpretation of the historical process. The new thesis, antithesis and synthesis are, however, never the same as the old ones. It would, therefore, be unwise to regard the irreligious man of the twentieth as of the same character as the irreligious man of the eighteenth century. He is the product of different conflicts; there are different elements in his composition.

It would be equally unwise for those who are convinced that the basis of the universe is spiritual to condemn the secularist temper of the modern world; rather they should try to understand it. Its fundamental causes have been analysed, albeit too briefly and inadequately, above. One must acknowledge that Freud was, at least partially, right. Much of what has gone under the name of religion has been a projection. The assumption of the existence of supernatural powers or a supernatural power has, to a great extent, been a creation of man's mind to escape from his own inadequacy and helplessness and to account for phenomena he could not understand. Now he has become more aware of the psychological processes which dictated this particular sort of projection. Not only that, as his knowledge of the universe has increased, to postulate the existence of a God has become no longer necessary to explain its workings; there are more likely hypotheses, he feels, to account for the nature of things. Even if the idea of God may still linger in his mind, the particular idea or image of God with which he is familiar no longer convinces. Finally, twentieth-century man no longer has the same sense of his own inadequacy and helplessness as his forebears had. Even though he is fearful of the possibility of nuclear war, he feels himself, as never before, the master of his fate, and is intent, by his own efforts, not only on creating a better world, but even on penetrating the farthest reaches of space. The technologist and the astronaut are the heroes and symbols of twentieth-century man.

Should we assume then that, as at the beginning of the Christian ěra the Mediterranean world saw the *Death of the Gods*, our own era will see, in Nietzsche's phrase, the *Death of God*? Are we entering on a period of world history in which the image of God will entirely fade from the minds of men and in which any religion which includes the idea of a transcendent God will disappear, except as a form of escapism for the ignorant, obscurantist and fainthearted? Let us not assume that until we have surveyed, analysed, asked questions. Sir Julian Huxley, who has been called the arch-priest of scientific humanism, in the article in the *Observer* under the title 'Religion without God' mentioned above, wrote these words:

There remains the fundamental mystery of existence, notably the existence of mind. . . . It remains true that many phenomena are charged with a magical quality of transcendent or even compulsive power over our minds, and introduce us to realms beyond ordinary experience. They merit a special designation: for want of a better, I use the term *divine*, though this quality of divinity is not supernatural but *transnatural.* The divinity is what man finds worthy of adoration, that which compels his awe.

This sense of the holy, the numinous, the divine, is part of our experience. What is its significance? What sort of validity may we attach to it? Whence does it originate? It is certainly *transnatural*, i.e. *immanent* in our inner experience and in the phenomenal world. Is it more than that? Is it also *transcendent, ultra-* or *supra-natural*, i.e. 'outside', 'other than', the time-space continuum of the phenomenal world? And if so, in what way? That is one of the most important issues which must be considered as this book proceeds. On it everything turns.

2

Perception and Knowledge

WHEN Father Kenelm Foster O.P. reviewed a book, *Towards a New Aristocracy*, which I wrote in 1943, and in which I described the formation of what I called a Company of Honour and Service, he concluded his review with these words:

As a story its climax is the Company of Honour and Service, a sort of modernist Grail (for boys) or Sodality which Dr Happold founded in 1935 at Bishop Wordsworth's School, Salisbury. This is his nucleus, his 'order', his new aristocracy, which is to permeate England: a little cohort of leaders, of seers, of doers.

What will they do? 'Possibilities' does not tell you precisely. In a general way it argues for this type of aristocracy and training, it gropes into the future, it urges the Higher Christianity. I am not jeering. Dr Happold really thinks that Christianity must get 'higher' by passing beyond creed and dogma; and then you can bring youth to the altar and dedicate it and sew the Cross of Sacrifice on its left shoulder.

Well, this is happening. It is a fact and a factor in our world, perhaps a growing one, perhaps dynamic. What shall I say? I put only three questions: (1) Granted an undogmatic 'faith' in that 'World of Being' from which moral values and the Company of Service derive, will not intellect strive to *define* this world? (2) Can *human* energy persist at all if it does not define its absolutes, reach clarity of truth? (3) Can this be done except on a basis of dogmatic credenda? The history of European intellect suggests an answer.

How right he was and how fair a criticism of my attitude at that time. How right, too, were the puzzled young people in Wells's novel: 'At the back of all there surely must be a creed, a fundamental statement.' Not only that, if it is to be acceptable to the deepest instincts of twentieth-century man, it must be 'in language which does not conflict with

33

every reality we know about the world.' I use the words, 'deepest instincts', deliberately, for it is a characteristic of our age that it has lost its direction posts. The condition of many people is that they do not know what they want; they only know that they want something which will give meaning to life. The fundamental questions remain and will. always remain: What is the nature of God, of the universe, of ourselves? We cannot escape the necessity to try to define the 'World of Being' and, for those for whom I am primarily writing this book, it must be in terms which they regard as intellectually honest. While one may rightly ask them to examine their 'realities', the answers given to the fundamental questions must not conflict with the realities they know about the world. To try and find answers which not only do not conflict with, but also spring out of, the realities which are the realities of twentieth-century man is the aim, however inadequately accomplished, of this book.

The basic issue with which we must start, is an epistemological one, i.e. the problem of knowledge, how do we know, what do we know, what is the validity of that which we think we know? These questions immediately give rise to another fundamental question: What is it that knows? Or, put in another way: What is the knower, that is myself, which knows?*

How do we know? There are five possible ways of knowing. There is first the knowledge of a material world outside ourselves which we gain through our senses. Next is the knowledge we have of our sensations and the knowledge which comes through introspection. Thirdly there is the knowledge we gain by the use of reason or intellect, which interrogates and interprets the first two types of knowledge and which is governed by the laws of logic. This is rational knowledge. Rational knowledge is, however, incomplete in

* For the sake of clarity I am compelled to cover here some of the ground I tried to cover in Section 4 of *Mysticism*.

itself and can only carry us a certain distance. In addition to the rational faculty men possess, in varying degrees, a faculty of intuition or insight. It is found particularly in seers, inventors, poets and other creative artists. Some have questioned whether knowledge gained through insight or intuition is valid knowledge. May it not be too much influenced by emotions, feelings and desires? The criterion is whether or not it satisfies the deepest parts of our being and whether or not it contradicts or supplements and illuminates rational knowledge. In the most highly developed minds rational and intuitive knowledge coalesce in complete harmony. Finally, there is the knowledge which is given through mystical experience at various levels. Here we are on more difficult ground. The mystics claim that through mystical experience they have direct and intimate contact with that which simply *is*. Though they themselves have a sense of complete certainty, they are not able to substantiate their claim rationally. Though there are some who question it, there is a strong case, however, for the validity of knowledge gained through mystical insight.

May we start with two statements? First, whatever it is, there is something which simply *IS*, an Ultimate Reality which is simply *there*. Even if it is not possible to demonstrate with certainty that the world which we think we know is not merely a construction of our own minds, we should still have to assume some sort of what Bertrand Russell calls 'sense data', which, impinging on our minds, create the picture of the world we see. The *IS* is still there apart from ourselves. Secondly, the starting point in the exploration of the nature of what *IS* cannot but be the fact of self-consciousness. Though I may be prepared to acknowledge that I know nothing else, and the world I think I know may be an illusion, of one thing I am certain, that *I*, for myself, am real, that *I* exist, and that *I* know that *I* exist, that, in short, *I* am *I*. If that is so, then I must assume that all the other selves I meet with in my daily life have the same sort of 'realness' which I feel I have. For practical purposes this is true. I myself, all the people I meet with and the world which is not myself, are all real. So long as I am alive, I have got to live with them.

But when I ask the question: What is this self, this *I* of which I am conscious, the problem becomes more difficult. It is possible to deny the existence of any continuing individual self, even my own self, at all. For when the nature of this self, which I think of *myself* is examined, all that is found is a constantly changing series of physical and psychological states, so that the *I* which I was a year ago is not the *I* I am now. That is true. Yet somehow it does not seem to be the whole truth. Even though we may not be able to explain it, we are conscious within ourselves of something more. It is, therefore, not unreasonable to take as hypothesis the Hindu belief that each one of us is really two selves, an ephemeral, phenomenal self, which is the self of which we are mainly conscious, and a 'greater self' which continues to be amid the slow changes of the organism, the flux of sensations, the dissipation of ideas and the fading of memories, and is our true immortal self. It will be necessary to examine more fully this conception of the two selves later; it does not necessarily involve a dualism or a 'ghost in the machine' thesis.

Thus, while it may be logically unsound to start with what seem to be such obvious statements as 'I exist', or 'I am I', and we ought merely to say, with the Buddhist philosopher, 'There is an existent', this existent, whatever it may be, is for me, as I am now, *myself*. Simply as a starting point we must assume the fact of self-consciousness; for, unless we are prepared to do so, we cannot start our exploration at all. There is no one to explore.

'Those who in the search for truth', wrote the eminent physicist, Sir Arthur Eddington, 'start from consciousness as a seat of self-knowledge, with interests and responsibilities not confined to the material plane, are just as much facing the hard facts of experience as those who start from consciousness as a device for reading the indications of spectroscopes and micrometers.'*

Through consciousness, then, I have experience of two worlds, an outer 'world', known to me through sense perception, and a 'world' within myself. I have an urge to try to understand both these worlds. I reason about them.

Reason is the instrument through which man interrogates and interprets his experience. A process of reasoning can, however, only take place as the result of experience, for without experience there would be nothing to reason about. Experience must, therefore, be regarded as the primary thing.

Now it is axiomatic that a person is only able to perceive that which, with his particular organs of perception, he is capable of perceiving; and the range of normal individual perception is limited. Thus no one perceives more than a fraction of that which is *there*. Secondly, the perception of each individual is selective; consciously or unconsciously he selects from his experience. Different people not only select different elements of their experience, but also interpret what they have selected in different ways. In every mind, moreover, there is an inherent bias of both selection and interpretation, dependent on disposition, heredity, environment and mental endowment. Finally, not only can the capacity of awareness be enlarged by training, but also normal perception can be extended by mechanical means. For instance, to unaided, natural perception a piece of Stilton cheese is lifeless; when it is put under a microscope, it is seen to be teeming with life.

It is, therefore, unreasonable to assume that that which one cannot perceive does not exist or that one's interpre-

* *The Nature of the Physical World* (C.U.P.).

tation of the meaning of even that which one can perceive is infallible.

> Look how the floor of heaven
> Is thick inlaid with patines of bright gold:
> There's not the smallest orb which thou beholdest
> But in his motion like an angel sings,
> Still quiring to the young-eyed cherubins;
> Such harmony is in immortal souls;
> But whilst this muddy vesture of decay
> Doth grossly close it in, we cannot hear it.

That you or I cannot hear clearly, or perhaps cannot hear at all, the harmonies of the world of spirit, does not prove that there is no celestial orchestra. It may simply mean that our receiving sets are defective, that, being human, we are closed in by 'this muddy vesture of decay'. Throughout the ages many have claimed with complete conviction that they have heard.

Unless he is merely a bundle of conditioned reflexes, in his acts of reason, man is, within certain limits, free to choose the logical categories he employs. He is free to decide on the experiences he will take as his starting point and which he will regard as valid. He is also free to choose the tools whereby he interrogates and interprets them. The validity of the data chosen as the starting point and of the apparatus selected for its examination cannot, as such, however, be rationally proved. Every speculation about the nature of reality is inevitably based on a primary act of *intellectual faith*, that is, an acceptance as the foundation of thinking of convictions which cannot be rationally demonstrated as certain. This primary act of faith, even when it is in part unconscious, is essentially an *intellectual* act, since it is a weighing up by the intellect of alternatives and a choice between different, perhaps conflicting, possibilities. There are other types of 'faith', which are not primarily intellectual but are based on intuitions, which have not had their origin in a process of rational thought.

Within the totality of human experience there have been, and are, two main kinds of consciousness, two modes of awareness, which open up different windows of apprehension, one typical of Western, the other of Eastern, modes of thought.

Our Western culture has tended to concentrate on the outward and active. European man has striven to find the truth primarily through the exercise of reason, by means of which he has believed that the meaning of the universe could be laid bare. His eyes have been turned outward to the phenomena of the material world, the nature and laws of which he believed could be discovered through observation, experiment and logical thought. His chief object has been, particularly during recent centuries, through knowledge to control nature and bend it to his will. Human history has meaning for him as the story of the conquest of nature by man through reason and science. Science and technology have been the supreme achievements of Western European civilization.

In the culture of the East the emphasis has tended to be far more on the inner and the passive. The deep truth of things, it has been believed, is not to be found through knowledge of the world of material phenomena, which is regarded as *maya*, i.e. appearance or illusion, and only in part through discursive thought, but through spiritual intuition, passivity and contemplation. To the followers of this path human history has seemed to have little or no significance, to be only a series of meaningless cycles, leading to no goal. Life is a prison house, from which the enlightened man will, through knowledge of the true nature of things, strive to escape.

Those cultures which have been animated by this theory of the nature of existence have often been distinguished by a deep fund of psychological and spiritual insight. They have not, however, been outstanding in scientific achievement; nor has there been present in them a strong urge towards social and material betterment.

When we say that these two types of consciousness are respectively typical of Western and Eastern cultures, we are writing in very general terms. One may perhaps be over-stressing the passive element in Eastern thought. There have been, moreover, throughout history all sorts of cross-fertilizations, variations, and balances between and within different cultures. What it is important to realize is that, because we are conditioned by our Western cultural heri-tage, we should not be tempted to regard them as mutually exclusive, or to consider our own way of looking at the world as necessarily better or more realistic. Rather these two attitudes of mind should be seen for what they are, complementary, two kinds of perception, two attitudes towards life, each with a validity of its own, each sup-plementing the other.

One cannot stress too strongly the extent to which our world-view has been conditioned by our mental history and development.

In recent centuries Western European thought-patterns have been dominated by that dualistic thinking which was expressed by Descartes in the seventeenth century when he drew the distinction between *res extensa*, matter extended in space, and *res cogitans*, the conscious mind standing over against and observing a world outside itself. This dualistic thinking is, however, not sacrosanct and there are in-dications that both religious and scientific thought are moving away from this Cartesian dualism.

In order to construct a picture of the universe out of our sensations and perceptions, mental operations are called for which Kant grouped together under the concept of *cate-gories*. The particular categories, space, time, number, personality, etc., which we use and which determine our world-view are, however, the result of a long and complicated mental development over the centuries. They cannot, therefore, be regarded as necessarily and always valid. If one should take the *pneuma* and *psyche* of much religious thinking or the *atman* and *karma* of Hindu psychology as the primary categories of experience, one's world-view would be different.

In the achievements of Western European civilization in the domain of science and its applications the mental tools whereby these achievements have been brought about have been analysis and logic. The result has been that the heirs of Western European culture have tended to regard these tools as the only valid tools of knowledge. Knowledge arising out of intuition and feeling has been regarded with some suspicion.

Yet Max Planck, one of the greatest pioneers of quantum physics, could write in his autobiography:

When the pioneer in science sends forth the groping fingers of his thoughts, he must have a vivid *intuitive* imagination, for new ideas are not generated by deduction, but by an artistically creative imagination. [The italics are mine.]

Another scientist, Alexis Carrel, particularly eminent in the field of medicine, wrote of intuition in similar terms:

Men of genius, in addition to their powers of observation and comprehension, possess other qualities, such as intuition and creative imagination. *Through intuition they learn things ignored by other men*, they perceive relations between seemingly isolated phenomena, they unconsciously feel the presence of the unknown treasure. All great men are endowed with intuition. *They know without analysis, without reasoning*, what is important for them to know. [Again, the italics are mine.]*

* *Man the Unknown* (Penguin Books).

Finally, in his *The Nature of the Physical World*, Eddington wrote:

> Our conception of the familiar table was an illusion. [He had previously shown how different the table of the physicist, made up of electrical charges in empty space, was from the solid table of commonsense perception.] To reach the reality of the table we need to be endowed with sense organs to weave images and illusions about it. And so it seems to me that the first step in a broader revelation to man must be the awakening of image-building in connection with the higher faculties of his nature, so that these are no longer blind alleys but open into a spiritual world, a world partly of illusion, no doubt, but in which he lives no less than in the world, also of illusion, revealed by the senses.

Thus, intuition must be accepted as a valid and all-important tool of knowledge of the truth of things. In a way it can be said to be the primary tool of knowledge, the great probe into the most profound secrets. The discoveries of intuition have, however, to be developed by means of logic. Not only that, there is danger of illusion if reliance is placed on intuition alone. Therefore, intuition must be brought before the bar of reason. Intuition and analysis must supplement each other.

Evolution, according to the thesis which Father Pierre Teilhard de Chardin puts forward in *The Phenomenon of Man*, may be seen as a movement from the very simple to the extremely complex, and an extension and enlargement of the psyche or consciousness. It is possible to assume the existence of a psyche, in an embryonic, undeveloped form, in every corpuscle. With the appearance of man, however, a new form of biological existence comes into being. It is characterized by the emergence of the power of reflection, of thought, with the result that the *within* becomes more and more the dominating evolutionary factor.

If this be a true interpretation of the evolution of life,

one may anticipate – though one must be prepared to think in terms of centuries, perhaps of millennia – that the evolutionary process will take the form of an emergence of an ever higher type of consciousness and awareness, an expanding interiorization and spiritualization of man, so that aspects of the universe will be opened up which are as yet hidden from or only faintly glimpsed by most men, but which have been more clearly discerned by that minority in whom interiorization and spirituality have been most highly developed, the poets, artists and musicians, the seers, saints and the mystics. In them intuition and imagination is found in its most perfected form.

3
Polarity, Unity, Totality, Evolution

BEFORE we go on to describe that transformation of the scientific world-view which inevitably determines the religious attitudes and ideas of twentieth-century man, it will be useful to set out certain key ideas, which have come out of my thought and experience, and which I shall take as the postulates of this book.

1. POLARITY AND UNITY

Let me go back to the second of those experiences in my room in Peterhouse in 1913, described in the Introduction. I have said that at the time, though I felt it contained the key to a secret, I did not know clearly what it meant. During the next two years I tried to express in verse its meaning as I then saw it. I will quote one example:

> Some sought a fair green tree,
> Whose roots in the breast of earth
> Have grown continually
> In the sequence of death and birth.

> Some knelt in the holy gloom
> Of the chapel of the Star,
> And longed for the quiet room
> Of a mansion dim and far.

> But they who longed for the kiss
> Of earth found the heavenly pool;
> And they who prayed for the bliss
> Of God found earth's bosom cool.

44

> For Earth is commingled with Heaven:
> In the damp and flowery sod
> Are God and His angels seven;
> And earth rests in the heart of God.

I now appreciate that what, very inadequately, I was try-ing to express in these verses was something which I can now grasp much more fully and completely, the mysterious and intimate co-inherence which exists between spirit and matter, between timelessness and time, a co-inherence which finds its superb expression in the Incarnation of Christ and is at the heart of the Christian dogma of Jesus Christ as true God and true man.

Some twenty years were to pass before I came across *The Vision of God* by that remarkable fifteenth-century figure, Nicholas of Cusa, at the same time a Cardinal of the Church, a great ecclesiastical statesman, an anticipator of modern science and the last of the medieval mystics. There at last I found, in his doctrine of the coincidence of contradictories (or opposites), not only a clear and precise expression of what I had already intuitively grasped, but also an extension of its meaning and significance. Let me quote some of his own words:

I have learnt that the place where Thou [i.e. God] art found unveiled is girt round with the coincidence of contradic-tories, and this is the wall of Paradise wherein Thou dost abide, the door whereof is guarded by the proud spirit of Reason, and, unless he is vanquished, the way will not be open. Thus 'tis beyond the coincidence of contradictories Thou mayest be seen and nowhere this side thereof.*

> This discord in the pact of things,
> This endless war twixt truth and truth,
> That singly hold, yet give the lie
> To him who seeks to yoke them both . . .

* Translated by E. G. Salter (Dent).

> Or is truth one without a flaw,
> And all things to each other turn,
> But the soul, sunken in desire,
> No longer can the links discern
> In glimmering of her smothered fire?*

So wrote the sixth-century philosopher-poet, Boethius. We live in a world of polar opposites which, except in so far as we can grasp the unity beyond them, condition the whole of our perception. For instance, we cannot grasp the idea of light except as the opposite of darkness, of hot except as the opposite of cold, of good except as the opposite of evil. Our perception of spatial and temporal relations is also of this polar character, above and below, within and without, before and after, earlier than and later than, and so on. These polar opposites are present not only in the whole of our conceptual thinking but also, unless and until we can rise beyond them, in our spiritual apprehension. Imprisoned as we are in a world of polar opposites, we are conscious both of an 'endless war twixt truth and truth' and also of a division in our souls. Our deepest longing is to break through the polar-opposites and to find again the Primal Meaning which we feel exists beyond phenomena, so that we may be restored to that Undivided Unity from which we spring, but which we have lost, and with which we long to be again united. This, however, necessitates passing beyond that rational approach which is effective in the examination and interpretation of material phenomena. This does not mean the abandonment of logical reason but the calling into play of another instrument of knowing, which can penetrate into spheres of reality which cannot be entered by means of discursive thinking. The door of the wall of Paradise wherein God, complete Reality, is found, is guarded by the proud spirit of Reason and 'unless he is

* *Medieval Latin Lyrics*, translated by Helen Waddell (Penguin Books).

vanquished the way will not be open'. And note, this was written, not by a man with a woolly mind, but by one of the greatest and most penetrating intellects of his age.

In his vision of the polar opposites and their resolution in that Primal Meaning and Undivided Unity, from which they sprang, Nicholas of Cusa does not stand alone. A similar vision had been glimpsed long before.

I found it in the Creation myth of the first chapters of Genesis. Here the parents of the human race dwell in the Garden of Eden, in which there are no opposites. They eat of the Tree of Knowledge of the polar-opposites of good and evil. The result is their expulsion from Paradise into the phenomenal world. In the Genesis myth the polarities are not resolved. Their resolution is described in the Christian story of Redemption, in which the Second Woman, Mary, reverses the choice of Eve, the First Woman; while the second Adam, the God-man, Jesus Christ, performs the act of reconciliation on the Tree of the Cross.

I found the same idea in the Taoist religious philosophy of ancient China. Here the phenomenal universe is envisaged as being brought into existence by a *coming out of Tao*, the ultimate Principle of Everything, through the pulling asunder of the polar-opposites. Out of Tao sprang the principles of phenomenal reality, the two poles of *yang* (light) and *yin* (darkness), which are evident throughout the whole of creation as we perceive it. The polar-opposites of *yang* and *yin*, though they have their origin in the undifferentiated unity of Tao, are, however, only active in the realm of phenomena.

Much the same sort of penetration is seen in the nondualistic thought of Hinduism, as one finds it enshrined in the Upanishads, where God is described as 'that which has no second'.

As early as the fifth century B.C., the Greek philosopher-scientist, Heraclitus, enunciated the double truth of the

47

state of flux which conditioned everything earthly and, over and against this flux, an unconditioned law whereby the opposites of earthly existence and thought were united.

It was, however, in the principle of complementarity which the quantum physicists of our own time have, as a result of their experiments, been compelled to adopt that I found the conception we have been discussing in an unexpected and particularly striking form.

It was with increasing excitement that, in 1953, I listened to Professor Philip Oppenheimer delivering his B.B.C. Reith lectures on *Science and the Common Understanding*.* He describes the principle of complementarity in these words:

> In its simplest form it is that an electron must sometimes be considered as a wave and sometimes as a particle. There is the same duality for all matter and for light. In a little subtler form this complementarity means that there are situations in which the position of an atomic object can be measured and defined and thought about without contradiction; and other situations in which this is not so, but in which qualities, such as energy or the impulse of the system, are defined and meaningful. The more nearly appropriate the first way of thinking is to a situation, the more wholly inappropriate the second.

It was even more startling when he went on to say:

> To what appear to be the simplest questions we will tend to give either no answer or an answer which will at first sight be reminiscent more of a strange catechism than of the straightforward affirmations of physical science. If we ask, for instance, whether the position of the electron remains the same, we must say 'No'; if we ask whether the position of the electron changes with time, we must say 'No'; if we ask whether the electron is at rest, we must say 'No'; if we ask whether it is in motion we must say 'No'.

* Published by O.U.P.

But surely, you may say, this is absurd. A thing must either move or be at rest; it cannot be both. Professor Oppenheimer goes on:

The Buddha has given such answers when interrogated as to the condition of man's self after death; but they are not familiar answers for the tradition of seventeenth- and eighteenth-century science.

They certainly are not; but listen again to Nicholas of Cusa. He is speaking, not about electrons, but about God:

Thou, Lord, dost stand and move at the same time, at the same time Thou dost proceed and rest . . . Wherefore Thou standest and proceedest and yet at the same time dost not stand and proceed.

The similarity of thinking and speaking of a fifteenth-century churchman and a twentieth-century atomic physicist is obvious. They are in the same continuum. Is there any relevance? While one must be wary of drawing unwarranted conclusions, there does appear to be a sort of relevance which, says Professor Oppenheimer, is 'a kind of analogy, often of great depth and scope, in which views which have been created or substantiated in some scientific enterprise are similar to those *which ought to be held with regard to metaphysical, epistemological, political or ethical problems.*' The italics are mine. Nicholas of Cusa went on:

Hence I observe how needful it is for me to enter into darkness, and to admit the coincidence of opposites beyond all grasp of reason and there to seek truth where impossibility meeteth me.

To what has all this led us? It may be put in this way. If our perception were such that we could see it, we should realize that behind and at the root of everything there is a unity, the Tao of ancient Chinese philosophy, the One in the all and the all in the One of the mystics. We, however, being what we are, can only grasp this unity in part, if at all.

49

Our perception is conditioned by the principle of polar-opposites. Yet there is something in us that impels us to believe that an ultimate synthesis exists if we could only attain it, an ultimate Truth, in which all opposites, all partial 'truths', which sometimes seem to contradict each other, are resolved and harmonized.

The existence of the polar opposites, not only in our perception and thinking, but also at the very heart of our spiritual and moral being, creates a 'discord in the pact of things', which at times can be painful. Intellectually, our desire is to find the unifying concepts. This desire is strongly evident in modern scientific thinking. It is found, for instance, in the *organismic conception* and the *general system theory* of Ludwig von Bertalanffy and others, which strives to find the unifying concepts not only in the special sciences, but also in the whole of scientific knowledge. Spiritually, there is an urge to reconcile the conflicting elements in our nature, not only the 'endless war twixt truth and truth', but also the endless war between the good and evil of which we are conscious within us.

From what has been written above it follows that the most complete unifying statement which can be made about reality will be not one statement, but two complementary statements, which together make up a more complete and exact statement. Let me give an example. In the religio-philosophical thought of Hinduism the basis of everything is Spirit, 'the undying, blazing Spirit, wherein lay hidden the world and all its creatures.'

Thus Hinduism says, *Matter is born in spirit*. In *The Biology of the Spirit*, Dr Edward Sinnott makes what looks like a completely opposite statement, *Spirit is born in matter*. When one examines these two apparently conflicting statements, it is seen that each is true in its particular setting. The first is a religio-philosophical statement, the second an evolutionary biological statement. Each is required to complete the other. So when Sir Julian Huxley writes: 'I believe that an equally drastic reorganisation of our religious thought is now becoming necessary, from a God-centred to an evolution-centred pattern', one would reply that the two patterns should be regarded as complementary.

The Something, within and beyond the polarities of human perception, which simply *is* has been called by many names with various shades of meaning. In general terms it is spoken of as Ultimate Reality or Ultimate Truth. Some philosophers call it the Absolute. For the religious it is God. Chinese metaphysicians call it Tao, Plotinus the One. For Hinduism it is Everlasting Spirit. For others Ultimate Reality is conceived as Mind, though in a much wider sense than our finite minds. Scientists use the concept of Energy, which cannot be known in itself, but only through its effects.

This Something which is the Is-ness of everything, is, however, in its completeness, concealed from human perception. It is the *Unknowable*, the *Inexpressible*, the *Unconditioned*. It is the *Mystery* which can only be known, at least intellectually, as an *image*, a *model*, an *approximation*. 'All we know of truth', wrote Nicholas of Cusa, 'is that absolute truth, such as it is, is beyond our reach. . . . The quiddity of things, which is ontological truth, is unattainable in its entirety; and though it has been the object of all philosophers, by none has it been found as it really is. The more profoundly we learn this lesson of ignorance, the closer we draw to truth itself.'*

2. TRUTH AND TRUTHS

We are thus led on to draw a distinction between *Truth* and *truths*. Each partial *truth* may be true within its own sphere, but be only a fragment of *Truth* in its fullness; and, owing to the limitations of human perception, there is not

* *Of Learned Ignorance* (*De Docta Ignorantia*), translated by Fr Germain Heron (Routledge & Kegan Paul).

seldom a conflict between different *truths*. Truthfulness within each different *truth* is determined by whether or not it conforms with the accepted criteria of truthfulness within its particular field. Thus, we speak of a statement as being scientifically, historically, mathematically or psychologically true if it conforms with the criteria scientists etc. have evolved as the criteria which determines what may be said to be true within their particular fields of knowledge. There is also a 'truth' of language, which will be considered more fully later, which may be rightly used to determine whether or not a statement can be said to be 'meaningful'.

Let us consider a particular instance, which is relevant to the theme of this book, the statement in the Creed, 'born of the Virgin Mary'. Can one in the light of modern knowledge say that one 'believes in' a virgin birth? Can the fact of such a birth be maintained as being true scientifically or historically? Normally a birth involves the fertilization of the womb of the female by the semen of the male. There may have been rare cases when conception has taken place without this fertilization. The evidence is, however, uncertain. The scientist is bound to say that the possibility of a virgin birth is, if not actually impossible, at least improbable. Allowing, however, the scientific possibility, what is the character of the historical evidence? Here the historian is bound to say that the documentary evidence available does not enable him to establish the fact of the Virgin Birth in accordance with the criteria of historical truth as accepted by historians. Is then the credal statement 'born of the Virgin Mary' a statement which one who is intellectually honest can no longer make? Not necessarily so. What may not be able to be established as either scientifically or historically true, may be regarded as *mythically* and *dogmatically* true.

When examined objectively, dogma is seen to be a complex of mythological, symbolic, metaphysical, psychological, mystical and, in the Christian creeds, historical elements. It is a translation into the terms of the intellect of intuitions which have been apprehended mystically, psychologically and intuitively. It is thus a particular sort of truth demanding a particular sort of language, which, like every other sort of language, has to be learnt, if it is to be rightly understood. Jung maintained that dogma could only be understood psychologically; while the Russian religious philosopher, Nicholas Berdyaev, defined it as the *symbolic* expression of mystical and eternal fact; it was not necessary, he said, to give the symbols a logical connotation or more than an implied metaphysical sanction.

Thus it is possible to say that one 'believes in' the Virgin Birth without any mental tension or reservation. This is true also of the dogma of the Assumption of the Blessed Virgin, promulgated in the Papal Bull, *Munificentissimus Deus*, the insight of which won such high praise from Dr C. E. Jung. It affirms that Mary as the Bride is united with the Son in the heavenly bridal chamber and as Sophia (Wisdom) is united with the Godhead. Thus the feminine principle is introduced into the Trinity.

> Virgin Mother, maiden peerless,
> Crowned with stars and clothed in gold,
> Woman chosen from all others
> In thine arms the Christ to hold.
>
> Thou the loom on which the Spirit
> Wove the Incarnate's robe of flesh,
> Human woof and warp of Godhead,
> Joined within a wondrous mesh.
>
> Mystic union! strange conjuncture!
> Immanent transcendency!
> Lo, the One thine arms upholdeth
> In His arms upholdeth thee.

When, in a libretto, written to be set to music, on the mystery of Christmas, I wrote this hymn to the Blessed Virgin, I did not pretend that I was using the language of science or history. I did feel, however, that I was expressing something essentially 'true' in the rich language of dogmatic symbolism.

3. THE TOTALITY OF EXPERIENCE

The task of science, as science, is the quantitative study of the material world. If it is to do its work, its thinking is necessarily in the way of time and history. It has its proved and effective methods within its own field, its own conception of what constitutes its own truth. But other aspects of time and history, which are no concern of the scientist *as scientist*, fall within our experience; and beyond them, also part of our experience, are immortal longings, intimations of something which is neither of time nor history.

If we are to reach the closest approximation to the synthesis in which all partial truths are contained, it is needful to accept, examine, and strive to coordinate all 'truths' and all human experience. It is unlikely that we shall be able to find the Truth by following one path only or by the aid of only one set of tools. If we are to grasp the Totality of things, it must surely be through the Totality of experience, not the experience of the scientist only, but also of the poet, artist, musician and mystic; not our own individual experience alone, nor the experience of our own Western European culture alone, but the total experience of the human race.

4. THE PRINCIPLE OF EVOLUTION

Everything within the space–time continuum in which we are contained is governed by the law of evolution. Everything evolves, plants, animals, human beings, thought, religion, institutions, perhaps, in so far as He manifests Himself within this continuum, God Himself. That fact, with all its implications, must be recognized and accepted.

The evolution of life on this planet has covered many millions of years. The appearance of *Homo sapiens*, a creature different from anything which had appeared before, capable of reflecting on his experience, and so gaining greater and greater control over his environment, dates back perhaps only half a million years. The era of written history, which has seen the emergence of the higher religions, covers only about six thousand years, a very long period in relation to an individual life, but in relation to the period of man's sojourn on this earth, minute.

Much is known of evolution in its physical aspects. One of its characteristics has been the presence of 'leaps', times when, by a process of long accumulation and adaptation, a new type suddenly emerges, suddenly, that is, in relation to cosmic time, different from anything that had appeared before and not inevitably contained in previous accumulations and adaptations. Elements combined in such a way as to produce a new creature and a new situation. Father Pierre Teilhard de Chardin uses the terms, *cosmogenesis*, *biogenesis*, and *noogenesis*, the genesis of the globe, the genesis of life, and, with the emergence of *Homo sapiens*, the genesis of thought. Within the stage of biogenesis several 'leaps' can be seen, for instance, the emergence of creatures which, unlike those which had preceded them, could live on land, and the emergence of mammals.

Our concern in this book, however, is with the mental and spiritual evolution of the human race. To what extent, and, more particularly, how, has the principle of evolution operated here? It is not easy to give precise answers. That the mental stature of mankind has evolved during the stage of noogenesis needs no demonstration. Though anthropologists have been able to tell us much about the character of primitive religion, it is impossible to say at what stage in the long period of pre-history a sense of the numinous and a 'beyond' appeared and how it evolved from its earlier embryonic forms. It is not until the stage of written history is reached that more precise information is possible. And compared with the half million years or so of man's sojourn on this planet, the six thousand years of written history is a very brief period. Within this period, however, it is possible to see one particular point when mankind seems to have leapt spiritually on to a new plane of vision and insight. It is possible that we, in our age, are in the midst of another such 'leap'.

This leap, in which spiritual vision passed on to a new plane and religious conceptions were recast and refined, took place during the first half of the millennium before the birth of Jesus Christ. It covered several centuries and occurred in several parts of the globe, taking different forms, each of which represented a revolutionary advance on the religious thought-patterns which had previously existed. In Palestine these centuries saw the appearance of the great Hebrew prophets, preaching a stern monotheism and social and individual righteousness. In Persia the teaching of Zoroaster took a similar form. Further East, there was in India a movement of great spiritual and philosophical depth. It arrived at two main assertions, that the source of everything which exists is Spirit, and that man, of his essential nature, is one with Everlasting Spirit. This same era saw also, in India, the rise of Buddhism, while China had its two sages, Confucius and Lao Tzu.

The appearance of a further religious insight some five hundred years later may or may not be regarded as a 'leap'. It may perhaps be seen rather as a significant extension and refinement of what had gone before, the idea of the divine-human figure, who is a Saviour and Redeemer and the

56

mediator between the unknowable Godhead and mankind. This Saviour-mediator idea is at this time expressed in the mythical* figure of the Krishna of the Hindu *Bhagavad Gita*,† in the significance given to the historical figure of Jesus in Christianity and in the Bodhisattva ideal in Mahayana Buddhism.

If one poses the question: is present day man more spiritually and morally mature than he was three thousand years ago, it is difficult to give a categorical 'yes' or 'no'. The millennial optimism and belief in inevitable, uninterrupted progress of my youth has proved to be an illusion.

There has clearly been, however, since the appearance of *Homo sapiens*, an enlargement and refinement of spiritual vision when favourable circumstances have obtained, and various cross-fertilizations of ideas and images, whereby insights which arose in different parts of the world coalesced, with, as a consequence, a gradual culminative hoarding of spiritual knowledge and experience. The result is that each successive era starts at a point different from that of those which preceded it. In view of the shortness of the historical time in which precise information is available there is little more that it is possible to say. In this process of enlargement, refinement, cross-fertilization and hoarding, mental, psychological and environmental elements have played a part. The particular combination of elements present has, to a great extent, determined what insights were capable of emergence and absorption into the corporate mentality in any particular era. When a specially favourable combination has existed, insights have been able to emerge in a way which would have been impossible under different circumstances.

---

* Some scholars maintain that there was a historical Krishna.

† There is some difference of opinion among scholars on the date of the Gita. I have adopted the view that it was completed in its present form between 100 B.C. and A.D. 200.

Moreover, in every age there have been geniuses whose spiritual perception was far in advance of that of ordinary men and whose vision, while influenced, was not limited by the thought-patterns of their times. The greatest of them were the founders of the higher religions. They are the mystics and seers, the pioneers in the spiritual adventure of mankind. They speak with the authority of those who know and their testimony may rightly be treated with the respect which is accorded to the pioneers in other branches of knowledge.

If we are prepared to acknowledge that the spiritual development of mankind has an evolutionary character, if, further, we are prepared to envisage the possibility that in our age an evolutionary 'leap' is taking place similar to that which took place in different parts of the globe three thousand years ago, what may we expect? We shall certainly expect that there will be a 'shattering of images'; but not necessarily the rejection of the insights of past ages. Rather may we not expect a gathering together of these old insights and their interfusion with the new knowledge of the universe and himself which modern man has gained? Out of this gathering and interfusion a new synthesis may emerge, demanding new concepts for its expression and new attitudes for its living.

It will be our next task to consider the impact of new knowledge and conceptions on the religious beliefs and attitudes of modern man. Before we start on this task, however, there is a question which may aptly be asked.

What is it that evolves? Is it possible to say with meaning that not only is man subject to a law of evolution, but so also, in a particular way, is God? To some the question may sound blasphemous; it has, however, been asked, and is still being asked. It raises profound theological and metaphysical issues, bound up with the nature of That we call God and the structure of the universe, and of man within that universe, and raises such questions as: What is the That which we name God? What is the universe, not merely as we see it with our particular range of perception, but in itself? What is the essential nature of man? And, most important, what is the relationship between God, the universe, and man within that universe? Does God stand over against the universe and man, or is He (or It), while 'above' and 'outside', also in some way 'within' both? If we are prepared to say with the Hindu that there is nothing which is not Spirit and that the universe is Its manifestation, in some sense partaking, at least in potentiality, of Its nature, we are asserting an interrelationship of Spirit and matter. Then, in so far as Spirit and matter coinhere within our space-time continuum, *within that continuum*, Spirit, God, may have to be said to 'evolve', in accordance with the law of evolution which dictates the pattern of that continuum. We shall then reach a point at which it is possible to say with meaning and reverence that God, though eternal Being *in Himself*, and therefore outside evolution, is *for us* in the process of formation all around us. Thus one may come to see God as the Heart of everything and evolution as a continuing process of Christification until everything is at length gathered together, reconciled and unified in the total Christ.*

* For further discussion, see Chapter 12.

4

The New Dimension of the Physical Universe

DURING my own lifetime a new dimension of the physical universe, which has resulted in a far-reaching transformation of the scientific world view, has been laid bare. That explanation of the nature of the universe, prevalent at the end of the nineteenth century, the explanation which is still that of popular imagination, has, as the result of new knowledge, proved to be untenable.

It would be an interesting task, were there space and time to do so, to trace the course of this scientific revolution in detail. It would tell of Dalton's enunciation, about 1800, of the theory of matter as made up of atoms; of the work of Clark Maxwell and Hertz in the latter half of the nineteenth century on the nature of light, which led to the electromagnetic theory of radiation; and of the experimental work of Rutherford, which revealed that the atom was made up of a positively charged nucleus, around which circled electrons, carrying negative charges, the atom itself being electrically neutral. It would go on to tell of Planck's Constant and of the work of Niels Bohr, which resulted in the abandonment of that form of visualization which conceived the atom in terms of a mechanical model.

A point was eventually reached when the universe of the quantum physicist could no longer be thought of as consisting of solid, unambiguous objects or as of something directly known. It was one, to quote Eddington, of 'unknowable actors executing unknowable actions'. This new scientific knowledge was neither of actors nor actions but of something of which the actors and the actions were a vehicle. It was *knowledge of a structure or pattern contained in the actions*, which could be described in a complex of mathematical symbols and pointer readings.

Since, because the things themselves were unknowable and unobservable, it was impossible to study *things*, Heisenberg laid down that what it was necessary to concentrate on was *relationships*. If these were established accurately, he argued, it would then be possible to predict *happenings*. Since it was also impossible to determine accurately both the position and momentum of an electron, he also maintained that *a principle of uncertainty* must be accepted. Further, since it did not prove possible to predict with certainty how an electron would behave under any particular circumstances, another physicist, Dirac, felt impelled to speak in terms of '*a definite distribution of probability* over a range of possible configurations of a system'. 'What physics', summed up Eddington, 'ultimately finds in the atom, or indeed in any other entity studied by physical means, is *the structure of a set of operations*'.

At the turn of the century the most widely held scientific view was that matter was solid and indestructible and that the universe was governed by laws which were inflexible and causally determined. As a result, however, not of abstract reasoning but of experimental exploration into the nature of the material world, scientists have now moved towards a new conception of matter, one not as something solid and indestructible, but as a concentrated form of energy. They are, further, no longer certain that the whole universe is governed by strict causality. A point has now been reached when it is not difficult to accept as a tenable hypothesis, perhaps as the most tenable hypothesis, that matter *is* energy, and that it is only energy that is indestructible.

No one, however, has seen or felt or experienced energy *as such*. The only means of knowing it is by its effects. In what sense then is it real? Or perhaps better, in what does its reality consist? Is it an idea existing only in our minds?

Is the basic reality of the universe, even the reality of that which we call the material universe, within, not outside, ourselves? Or is the ultimate reality to be found in some sort of relationship between what is within and what is without us? Such speculation can no longer be regarded as fantastic. Whatever the extent to which one is prepared to push the argument, this, at least, is true. The universe can be no longer thought of as made up of some sort of *stuff*, which can in any sense be *known*. Our knowledge is a knowledge of a *pattern of actions, the structure of a set of operations*. We must be content to study *relationships* in order to be in the position to predict the likelihood of *happenings*.

Thus, the *absolute object* of the older science has disappeared. In making that statement we are not denying the existence of an objective world. There is nothing in quantum physics which compels us to deny the reality of an objective world over and against ourselves; though we have to change our ideas about what it is. What is meant is that we can no longer think in terms of an object which is completely definable, unambiguous and perceivable.

The nature of time has always been one of the puzzles which has, down the ages, intrigued thinking men. What is t? Does it exist in its own right? Is it an illusion?

Einstein's Theory of Relativity, which has so profoundly influenced the scientific thinking of our era, was, in effect, a new statement on the meaning of space and time, based on the impossibility of determining absolute motion.

When we consider the whole universe, we are obliged to accept a whole series of space-frames, in which not only distances, but also magnetic forces, acceleration, etc. are relative to different observers. Thus, we are led to a picture of the universe as one of a multi-dimensional space–time continuum, space–time being a fusion of the concepts of space and time, a continuum a continuous series of component parts, passing into one another.

As in quantum physics we saw the disappearance of the absolute object, now, in the Theory of Relativity, we are bidden to abandon the idea of *absolute time*. It has become no longer possible to think of the whole of three-dimensional space passing simultaneously, moment by moment, through time. Instead we are compelled to think in terms of a four-dimensional universe, in which time is one of the dimensions.

Indeed, time appears to have no existence except in relation to particular reference systems. The universe considered in abstraction simply *is*, a multiplicity of points which only begin to form stretches of time when the human mind provides a reference system. In his Eddington Memorial lecture, *Time and Universe for the Scientific Conscience*, it was possible for Dr Martin Johnson to suggest that to ask, scientifically, whether the universe had a beginning, at a given epoch, or has existed always, is to be answered either way according to what kind of time-scale we select. It would seem that the universe in itself is timeless.

Before we examine the significance of this new knowledge of the physical universe, let us consider the new dimension of the spiritual universe, laid bare by the psychologists.

5

The New Dimension of the Spiritual Universe

THE laying bare of a new dimension of the spiritual universe has been the work of the depth-psychologists. The two outstanding figures have been Sigmund Freud and C. E. Jung.

The fundamental discovery of depth-psychology was that, in addition to the conscious surface mind, i.e. that part of a man which thinks and wills, and over which he has a greater or lesser degree of control, there is in everyone an *unconscious*, about which he has little knowledge and over which he has little or no control, but which profoundly influences his attitudes, thoughts and actions. The whole consciousness of a man has been compared to an ocean, in which consciousness, that part of a man which wills and thinks, is an island appearing above the surface of the water. The simile of an iceberg has been sometimes used, the conscious being the smaller part of it which appears above the surface. Directly below the surface, according to Jung, is the *personal unconscious*. This consists of (to quote his own words) 'what has been forgotten or repressed, and of sublimary perceptions, thoughts or feelings of any sort'. As a result of his observing that certain symbols were found all over the world, and that similar symbols emerged in myths, in dreams and in numerous other forms, Jung found himself compelled to postulate, in addition to the personal unconscious, a *collective unconscious*, which everywhere manifested itself in similar ways, assumed similar patterns and obeyed similar laws. The collective unconscious, in Jung's theory, consists of the inheritance of psychic experiences, not of one individual only, but of all mankind. Though there are differences of conception, it has affinities with the Universal Soul of Plotinus and, possibly, of Hinduism.

64

Psychology, and more especially depth-psychology, developing as it did under the influence of the materialistic philosophy of the nineteenth century, has tended to rationalize the religious instinct in man and to attribute it to causes which could be explained in materialistic terms. This is the point of view found in Freud's *The Future of an Illusion*. To Freud religion appeared as the rationalization of urges which were fundamentally 'sexual'; he gives the term an extended meaning from that of the normal.

The whole personality, in Freudian psychological concepts, is made up of the *id*, the natural self, which is a mixture of feelings of need, images of satisfaction and instinctive cravings; the *ego*, a compound of instincts and knowledge, gained by contact with the real world; and the *super-ego*, which, according to Freud, arises out of the infant's early psychological development and which becomes the restraining, forbidding element in his personality. To these three elements must be added the *ego-ideal*, which represents what a person would like to become. Throughout life there is a perpetual conflict between these elements of the personality and a constant effort to reach a satisfactory balance between them. For instance, if the *id* conquers the *ego* against the wishes of the *super-ego*, a sense of guilt arises.

As hypotheses, based on empirical scientific observation, to account for psychological phenomena, Freud's concepts are useful. They can be used with good effect in the examination and understanding of some of the processes of religious development. For instance, the account, given by St Paul, in the Epistle to the Romans, of his own religious conflict and its resolution can be seen as a religio-psychological process, whereby the dominance of the *super-ego* was overcome and St Paul was enabled to make the transition from a religious faith based on fear to one based on confidence and love. Such an analysis in no way invalidates the religious authenticity of the experience; it merely describes it in psychological terms.

Freud's interpretation of his own findings was, however, anti-religious. To him religion appeared as an illusory rationalization of unconscious wishes, as a projection to compensate for an infantile sense of helplessness. God was a projection of the infantile father-image, a fantasy-substitute for an actual, and not altogether satisfactory, father. For him 'sexuality', centred in the 'incest-wish', was the basic, dominant psychological factor, and this inherent 'sexuality' explained man's desire for union with God.

Jung's study of comparative religion, however, led him to a different interpretation. He found he was being presented by his patients in the course of his clinical work with symbols which he recognized as universal symbols found everywhere, in every age and in all parts of the world, for the creative and undifferentiated Divinity. This led him to conclude that *libido*, that is, the basic psychological urge, was not, as Freud had concluded, solely, or even primarily, sexual, but was a fund of undifferentiated energy. Eventually he came to see the many manifestations of *libido* as innate aspirations after God, corresponding to what the theologians call a *naturale desiderium* for God.

In *God and the Unconscious** Father Victor White sums up Jung's interpretation as follows:

Behind submerged 'memories' of events in the individual's life there lies a racial heritage manifested in archetypal figures. Behind the particularised mother's womb lies the archetypal womb of the Great Mother of all living; behind the physical father the archetypal Father; behind the child the *puer aeternus*; behind the particular manifestation of the procreative sexual *libido* lies the universal and re-creative Spirit. The second of all the pairs appears now, not as a fantasy-substitute for the first; but rather does the first appear

* Published by the Harvill Press.

as a particular manifestation and symbol of the second. The way is now open for us, for instance, no longer to conceive God as a substitute for the physical father, but rather the physical father as the infant's first substitute for God, the generic prior bearer of the image of the All-Father.

To some psychologists the unconscious had seemed to be a kind of cesspool, into which was poured everything that was nasty and unpleasant in experience, and which the conscious wanted to get rid of. That that is at least partly true of the personal unconscious Jung agreed, but he took the view that it was not the whole story, and in doing so made his most important contribution to the understanding of the religious instinct in mankind. He argued that the unconscious, and more particularly the collective unconscious, was the fount from which the deepest insights, the most profound wisdom of mankind sprang, in short, that the spiritual urge in man lay in the unconscious.

To make this clear let us briefly examine two of the fundamental elements in Jung's psychology. The first is his theory of the *archetypes of the collective unconscious*. What are these archetypes? They are not innate, inherited images; rather they are *dispositions to form images and symbols*. Jung calls the archetypes 'the organs of the prerational psyche'. 'Just as our physical organs are the result of a long process of development,' he wrote, 'so the archetypes are the outcome of all human experience, from right back in its earliest dark beginnings. Nor are they dead: for they live on as systems of reaction and disposition which determine life in an invisible, but all the more effective, manner.' So in the same way as a person who offends against the laws of the physical organs becomes physically ill, so anyone who offends against the laws of the archetypes becomes psychologically ill; he becomes a sick soul. If this be the case, we have an explanation of the sickness of our age.

Archetypes may thus be thought of as centres of energy of

immense power. Energy, as we have seen, cannot be known in itself, but only through what it does. So it is with the archetypes of the collective unconscious. They cannot be known of themselves, but only through the symbols which are their manifestation.

Symbols, what are they? What is their significance? More will have to be written later, but something must be said here. A symbol is not something which is purposely thought out, as is, for instance, a parable or an allegory. Symbols *happen*. They cannot be adequately translated into rational concepts; nor can such translations, if made, exhaust their meaning. A symbol is a picture of something which is felt to be truly real, but which cannot be grasped intellectually. We can feel that a symbol has meaning, indeed most profound meaning, yet we cannot put into words exactly how or why. Not only that, symbols are ambivalent, they act differently on and convey different meanings to different people. A symbol acts on the hearer or seer in such a way that it arouses in him feelings of awe or fear or love; it shifts his centre of awareness, so that things are perceived in a different light; it changes his values. It has thus a dynamic quality.

In the study of religion there are found certain symbols which constantly occur. They are not peculiar to any one religion. Such symbols are the divine Mother and Child, the divine Hero or Saviour, who is slain and rises again, the Cross, the Tree, the Fish.* Such symbols are not comprehensible or explainable at the level of rational thought. According to Jung's theory, they are archetypal symbols, enshrining the deepest spiritual wisdom of the human race.

The second fundamental element in Jung's psychology is his concept of the *self*. It is a difficult concept to understand, for, as the term is employed by Jung, it does not mean what is normally understood by the self, i.e. the individual

* For a very full discussion of the Fish symbol, see Jung: *Aion*.

personality. Nor, though it appears to have affinities, is it exactly synonymous with the 'self' of Hindu and Buddhist religious psychology. Jung defines the self as 'the archetypal image that leads out of polarity to the union of both partial systems through a common mid-point'. Since the self itself is an archetype, it cannot be rationally known; it can only be known through the symbols which are the manifestations of its archetypal energy. Jung sometimes calls it the *centre of the psyche*, sometimes the *periphery*, at other times the *whole*.

The fundamental idea which must be appreciated is that the self is the archetypal image which leads out of polarity. As, in the course of his work as a psychologist, Jung examined the inner happenings in the psyches of those he treated – and he found the same thing whether they were sick or healthy – he discovered that symbols emerged which he grouped under what he called *the reconciling symbol*. This reconciling symbol revealed the inner purpose deep down in the soul of the patient, the end towards which it was striving, and the failure to reach which made it feel at variance with itself. This inner disharmony is known to most of us; we feel that we are not true to our 'real selves'. Not only do we feel a lack of harmony in ourselves, we feel also a discord at the very heart of all things earthly. It is the deepest desire of men to find the reconciling symbol, to resolve the discords of which they are conscious, to pass from polarity to unity. This reconciling symbol Jung calls the symbol of the archetype of the self.

6

The Transformation of the Scientific World-View, and its Impact on Religious Thought

To what conclusions is our study of these new dimensions of the physical and spiritual universes leading us? It is not the function of the scientist, as scientist, to assume the cloak of the metaphysician or theologian. Physics – and what is true of physics, though there may be differences in objectives and techniques, is true of all the sciences – is the quantitative study of sense-data. Its concern is solely with the physical world. The twentieth-century physicist's picture of the universe is a particular mode of reacting to externals, a description of the pattern of a set of operations. His attention is, and must be, if he is to be a true scientist, fixed on 'the aggregate of observables capable of being symbolized in equations whose terms are not to be interrogated for "meaning".' It is not permissible for him to introduce a *deus ex machina* to explain what he cannot explain in the light of his scientific knowledge. Scientific truthfulness is a special sort of truthfulness, the truthfulness of the scientist in his own scientific domain. It is a beautiful form of truthfulness, characterized by a deep integrity and an austere beauty. Scientific knowledge is, however, knowledge within a defined and limited sphere. The scientist is, as scientist, as he himself acknowledges, on religious and metaphysical issues neutral.

The psychologist, as psychologist, is thus concerned solely with observables; his language is the language of psychology, not of metaphysics or theology. It is not perhaps surprising that some of his critics have accused Jung of equating the *self* with God, or that Father Teilhard's *The Phenomenon of Man* has been criticized as passing, in its later sections, into speculations which are *scientifically* illegitimate. Jung has made it crystal clear that he had no intention of equating the *self* with God. In one of his letters he wrote: 'How on earth did you get the idea that I could replace God – and with a concept at that. . . . This "self" can never take the place of God, though it may [and here he *is* using a theological term], perhaps, be a receptacle of the divine grace.'

Psychologically it is not possible to establish the difference between the 'image' of God in the soul and God Himself. When we speak of the God-image in the soul we are using the language of examinable experience; we are not necessarily making any theological pronouncement on the existence and nature of God. Similarly when St Paul says, 'I live, yet not I, but Christ liveth in me', he is describing what was for him a very real and convincing religious experience, the sense of the presence of Christ within him in so intense a form that his old *ego* had ceased to exist and had become Christ, in terms of the Christ-symbol. But when we speak of the Christ-symbol, in this way, we are speaking psychologically; we are not necessarily making any theological statement on the nature of Christ Himself.

Nevertheless, in one of his letters Jung wrote:

Christ in us and we in Him! Why should the activity of God and the presence of the Son of Man within us not be real and observable? Every day I am thankful to God that I have been allowed to experience the reality of the Divine Image within me.

Real and observable! These are the significant words. A new vision of our inner world is opened up. We are presented not with a revelation which can only be accepted by an act of unreasoning faith, nor with an inner experience which we may fear is delusion, but with an explorable spiritual terrain, which can be examined and interpreted before the bar of reason.

Thus, twentieth-century man has been led by the explorations of physicists and psychologists into a new dimension of a physico-spiritual universe. His world can no longer be the world of nineteenth-century science; his universe can no longer be thought of as made of solid stuff, one in which there seemed no room for 'spirit'. It has dissolved into energy, which cannot be known of itself but only by its effects. Indeed, the universe may be said to have become, without too great a stretching of the meaning of the term, a 'spiritual' universe. Scientists no longer consider it inconceivable, indeed it seems to fit in with their experience, both as men and scientists, that in those regions of personality which lie outside the orbit of normal consciousness (and there are such) the categories of time and space may be inappropriate and that man in his completeness dwells in a realm which embraces an infinity which cannot be rationally known. The world of normal experience may be in part 'illusion', not in the sense that it does not exist, but that what we perceive is a particular mental construction, determined by the particular range of our perceptions, and only a fragment of a greater whole.

Further, it has become evident that our apprehension of the sum-total of reality is carried out only in part by the rational mind, that much of it comes out of the unconscious. Such knowledge as we have of spiritual reality may come, not primarily through our senses, nor through the operation of our conscious rational minds, but from depths of our being which have as yet only been partially explored, a knowledge received in symbols, which appear differently to different people, and can only partially be translated into intellectual concepts. That is not, however, to say that intuitive spiritual awareness is irrational. Since the operations of the psyche are 'real and observable', they can be examined rationally, so that there can be in a fully integrated personality a fertile interplay of spiritual intuition and rational thought, out of which may come a 'spiritualized rationalism', which is, in a real sense, an extension of perceptive awareness.

If we accept as valid those basic principles which have been set out earlier in this book, e.g. that there is a unity of everything, even though we may not always, owing to the polar nature of human perception, be able to see it, that in order to arrive at the most complete truth we are capable of reaching in our present state of evolution we must embrace and yet pass beyond all partial truths, that to grasp the totality of things we must gather into our thinking the totality of human experience, the sort of relevance of which Professor Oppenheimer spoke is what we should expect to, and do indeed, find. We may be compelled to go further and declare that while science, *as science*, must confine itself to its own particular 'truth', it does in fact contain within itself an, at least implicit, metaphysic and theology.

At the very least, may it not be true to say that our apprehension of religious truth, *at the level of intellect*, has definite affinities with the scientist's apprehension of his truth? Are we not in fact compelled to accept that we are dealing with *unknowable actors executing unknowable* (or at least only partially knowable) *actions*, and is not our knowledge, in reality, a *knowledge of a structure or pattern contained in the actions*? May we not have to be content, for practical purposes, to study *relationships* in order to be in a position to predict *happenings*? Do we know, at the level of intellect, or, in our personal living and attitudes, do we need to know, more than the *structure of a set of operations*, the operations of the Divine in the world and in ourselves?

7
The Quest of Being:
The Existentialist Pilgrimage

No one who has not had the opportunity to study it can realize the great variety and richness of the philosophical and religious thought of our century. Had this book been conceived on a larger scale it would have been interesting to survey it in detail. One would have had to tell of the Absolute Idealism of F. H. Bradley, of the various philosophies of the Spirit, of the anthropological approach to religion of Frazer in *The Golden Bough* and of the psychological interpretations of Freud and Jung. One would have had to go on to consider inquiries into the relationship of theology, history and culture, as they are found in the works of Spengler, Croce, Gentile, Collingwood and Toynbee, as well as Schweitzer's 'quest of the historical Jesus' and the historico-mystical approach to religion of Baron von Hügel. Into our picture would have had to come the vitalism of Bergson, the phenomenological approach of Rudolf Otto and Eliade, the realism of Moore, Russell, Broad and Whitehead, and the significant writings of the Russian Nicholas Berdyaev. Space would have had to be given to the revival of the Thomist philosophy in the Roman Catholic Church and to the influential theology of the Word of Karl Barth.

The work of some of those mentioned above is described or referred to in various parts of this book. It is unnecessary for our purpose to do more. For those who would wish to go further, there is available the brilliantly clear, and almost encyclopaedic, *Twentieth Century Religious Thought* by Professor John Macquarrie.*

* Published by the S.C.M. Press. I personally have found this book not only of profound interest, but also of great value in writing this book, especially this and the following chapter.

Two aspects of current philosophical and religious thought, however, call for reasonably full treatment, e.g. that complex of religio-philosophical ideas known as Existentialism, and the rejection of metaphysics and the concentration on problems of language by the Logical Empiricists.

It is not easy to give a short and precise definition of Existentialism, for it has no body of generally accepted doctrines. It embraces the atheistic pessimism of Jean-Paul Sartre and the Catholicism of Gabriel Marcel. It may be defined as a particular religio-philosophical attitude, a method of approaching the mystery of reality, particularly the reality of man himself. One might aptly define this 'existentialist pilgrimage' as 'man in search of his soul'; the title which Jung gave to one of his books. It can be seen as a manifestation of the mood of current thinking and as a revolt against that superficial intellectualism which has characterized so much metaphysical thought. For this reason it has been unfairly criticized as being irrational and subjective.

The existentialist method is to begin by interrogating 'existence', by which is meant the kind of 'being' that belongs to man in his concrete living. Its command is, thus, a very ancient one, 'Know thyself'.

When one considers human existence as it is found in concrete living, what does one find? First of all, it is seen to be a threefold *encounter*, the encounter of what one knows as 'oneself' with a phenomenal world, with other selves and with a 'something other', which is not oneself, or the phenomenal world or another self.

Secondly, human existence has the character of what Martin Heidegger calls *thrownness*, that is, man is 'thrown' into a situation which he did not choose and which he does not control. The possibilities open to him at any time are conditioned by such factors as his race, his historical situation, his environment, his natural endowments, etc. He does not know where he came from or whither he is going. This gives rise to what Heidegger calls by the rather obscure word, *anxiety*, a mood in which a man is acutely conscious of a discord both in the world and in himself; an *anxiety* from which he longs to escape. In its most acute form this mood of anxiety may result in a feeling of the complete meaninglessness of everything. This mood is clearly revealed in much current drama; it is particularly vivid in, for instance, Beckett's *Waiting for Godot*.

From this 'anxiety' there are two ways of escape open. The first is to lose oneself by absorption in the world, in work, in people, in things, or, worse still, to become absorbed in the impersonal, anonymous existence of the mass, which is a shedding of all responsibility for anything, including oneself. This way, however, leads only into *inauthentic* existence and offers no ultimate escape.

The second way is to enter into an *authentic* existence, in which one takes into oneself the whole situation as it exists in the world and in oneself, with all its finitude, discords and sin. It is an attitude of complete acceptance of every possibility in existence, including death, which can appear as the shattering of all existence.

Heidegger's philosophy of authentic existence is a definitely religious one. It has affinities with the Abandonment to the Divine Providence of the eighteenth-century Jesuit, Father Pierre de Caussade. It was, as we shall see later, the way chosen by Jesus Christ.

Heidegger did not stop at interpreting existence only in its guise of an encounter of the self with that which is other than self. He pushed forward from the consideration of man's being to the consideration of 'being-in-itself'. Being-in-itself is not, however, he argued, an entity in the way man is an existent entity. It is not an 'object' which man, as subject, can survey. For him to penetrate to the meaning of being-in-itself a particular sort of thinking is called for, a particular sort of intellectual and spiritual submission and response. When this submission and response is made something happens. There is an essential and intimate relationship between man and being-in-itself so that, when the response is made, there is a reciprocal response from being-in-itself. Thus Heidegger's being-in-itself is what a religious person means by God, not, however, God thought of as standing over against man, but the God of the mystics such as Meister Eckhart, who said: 'The knower and the known are one. Simple people imagine that they should see God, as if He stood there and they here. God and I, we are one in knowledge.'

I have given a good deal of space to the philosophy of Martin Heidegger, possibly the most profound of existentialist thinkers, since by doing so, it has been possible to set out some of the basic features of existentialism. It will be useful, however, to consider other existentialist thinkers, both to fill out our picture and also to see how a similar type of approach has resulted in different existential responses in men of different spirituality and mentality, thrown into different environments.

First, Karl Jaspers. Karl Jaspers recognized three areas of being. There is, first, that realm of being which is capable of being objectified. In this realm he included not only the physical objects of the phenomenal world, but also human ideas, activities and institutions, in so far as these are regarded as over and against the observing ego. Secondly, there is our own distinctive kind of being, you and I as we are aware of ourselves. Thirdly, there is what he called *Transcendence*, which is Being-in-itself. Thus man's being is seen as encompassed by the being of the world and by Transcendence, i.e. that which is not the world. But how are they connected? And how is man's relation to *Transcendence* revealed to him? It can happen in more than one way, but, according to Jaspers, it happens when a man finds himself in what he calls a 'limit-situation', that is, when he finds himself 'at the end of his tether', when his sense of self-sufficiency has gone. It is then that he becomes aware of *Transcendence*, not as something standing over against himself, nor as contained within himself, but as something which is neither subject nor object, but has the nature of both. The recognition of the Transcendent, which is God, brings a man into contact with his authentic self. Here Jaspers' doctrine has marked affinities with that of the Hindu Vedanta; and indeed he regarded that period of man's history in the first millennium before the birth of Christ, which has been described earlier, as the most fertile and significant in the development of mankind.

There is a richness and penetration in the thought of the French Catholic, Gabriel Marcel. Three elements of particular interest stand out in his philosophy. The first is his 'metaphysic of hope', which he connects up with the very important distinction he makes between *mysteries* and *problems*. We tackle a problem, say a problem of mathematics or of science, from outside and our solution must be capable of empirical verification. A *mystery*, on the other hand, cannot be apprehended from outside. To grasp it, though one may subject it to analysis, one must be involved in it, in such a way that the subject-object relationship is transcended. Hope is such a mystery: so are other elements of experience, such as love. Their validity cannot be rationally demonstrated, they can only be grasped by a sort of direct inner awareness.

The second is the distinction Marcel makes between *having* and *being*. *Having* is a relationship which is external and egocentric; a relationship to objects outside ourselves and in which we have no deep involvement and which we use for our own purposes. We try to possess them, to get power over them, so that we may exploit or use them.

These 'objects' may be material things; they may be other people. They may even be, and this is important to realize if one is to attain to the deepest spiritual awareness, ideas. Yet concentration on having can never give satisfaction. The Buddha said this very clearly, when he attributed the whole of human suffering to 'desire'. The instinct of having is always with us; only the saints escape from it. It can, however, be transformed into *being*. When that happens there is a different relationship. The sharp distinction between self and what is not self is transcended. The attitude of narrow egocentricity gives place to one of reciprocity.

The third interesting element in Marcel's philosophy – and here he has kinship with Martin Buber – is his stress on the significance of *community* in human existence. We do not live as isolated individuals, we are perpetually, whether we want it or not, involved with other people. This was, for Sartre, part of the tragedy of human existence. For it led to infinite frustrations and unhappiness through the clash and conflict with other personalities, with whom one could not come to terms. In that terrible play, *Huis Clos*, he sums up the whole tragedy in a single phrase: 'Hell is other people'; and from that hell, for Sartre, there is no exit.

To Marcel, however, it was different, because he saw that it was possible for man to pass out of his attitude of having to one of being. This changed his attitude towards and relationship with other people and led to the emergence of the virtue he called 'fidelity', which had its origin in something greater than itself, in the love and self-giving of God. Thus the transcending of a narrow egocentric existence inevitably led on, according to Marcel, to a realization of the Being of God.

Lavelle's philosophy is similar to that of Marcel and, on some points, supplements it. One cannot discover self, he maintained, without at the same time discovering the total presence of being. True awareness is the discovery of participation in being. Everything that exists exists through its participation in that infinite Being which is God. This cannot be known, however, by rational thought but only by participation in infinite Being through an act of intuitive awareness.

It will be useful at this stage to stress certain points which emerge from what has already been written.

1. In some of these existentialist philosophies the impact of the spiritual and temporal crisis of our age is clearly evident. It is seen, for instance, in Heidegger's analysis of *anxiety*, which under stress leads to the mood of nothingness, the realization of what seems to be the total meaninglessness of everything, so that it is impossible to say 'Yes' to life. From it there appears to be no escape. It is seen, too, in Jaspers' doctrine of the *limit-situation*, the situation when a man finds himself at the end of his tether. Unless a way of escape can be found the descent into the trough of inauthentic existence is unavoidable.

2. Though existentialism starts out with the problem of human existence, where existence is understood as the kind of being which belongs to man in his concrete living, it was impossible for it to avoid going on to the consideration of the nature of being-in-itself. Though its method differed from that of earlier philosophers of being, who discussed the nature of being in isolation from actual human beings, nevertheless some, at least, of the existentialist philosophers regarded themselves as engaged in an ontological quest, that is, they wished to penetrate to the essence of things, to being in the abstract. And this was possible since, as Heidegger expressed it, 'man is a clearing in being, the locus where being is lit up and becomes unconcealed'. Because of this, not only their thought, but often also their language becomes mystical; indeed Heidegger's description of the sort of thinking needed to penetrate to the meaning of being-in-itself is a description of what we shall term a

movement into the realm of the mystical. Anyone who is acquainted with the literature of mysticism will have seen this already.

This is evident in the two existentialist theologians we shall now consider, Rudolf Bultmann and Paul Tillich, implicit, perhaps, in Bultmann, but quite open in Tillich, who has been influenced by Meister Eckhart; it is possible with exactness to speak of Tillich's religious philosophy as a mystical philosophy of the Unconditioned.

Bultmann's main field was in New Testament studies. Like Karl Barth he reacted against the nineteenth-century 'Jesus of history' school. His preoccupation with 'form criticism' led him to a very sceptical view of the historicity of the New Testament documents. What he saw in these documents was the story of an *encounter*, the encounter of Jesus and his disciples, which led to involvement and commitment and the birth of a 'new existence', in existentialist language, the story of a group of men who through Jesus passed from inauthentic to authentic existence.

Bultmann rejected any theology which involved a consideration of the 'natures' of Christ, such as is found in the Chalcedon Declaration of Faith. God, he maintained, cannot be known intellectually; He can be known only through an inner experience of His self-giving, i.e. through a God-for-me experience, which leads out of inauthentic into authentic existence. This is set out in the New Testament story in the form of a *kergyma*, i.e. in the form of a 'divine word' addressed to man. The *kergyma* is, however, concealed from contemporary man because it is expressed in the form of 'myths', which belong to a pre-scientific worldview. It is, therefore, necessary to 'demythologize' the New Testament story, so that, in a form free from myth, the understanding of existence, contained in the *kergyma*, may become clear and relevant once more.

Paul Tillich's thinking has an existentialist basis. What he does is to take the existential situation of man and the *kergyma* of the Christian revelation and to try to 'correlate' the questions implicit in the existential situation with the answers given in the *kergyma*.

Tillich holds that man's preoccupation with the idea of God springs out of his sense of his own finitude. It is, however, impossible to have a sense of finitude unless at the same time a sense of its polar opposite, infinity, is also contained in his experience. By his very nature man cannot find his rest in the finite; he must, as soon as he becomes spiritually awakened, stretch out towards the unconditioned, the absolute, the ultimate ground of being; this is bound to be his 'ultimate concern'. He has many concerns, bound up with his earthly existence. All these have, however, the nature of 'objects'; they are set over against him. The genuine ultimate must transcend this subject-object relationship and can, therefore, only be found by participation in it. This Ultimate, which alone we can call God, cannot be an 'object'; it must be infinitely above all existent objects, it is Being itself.

The identification of God with Being itself, or with the ground or power of being, makes it impossible to think, however, of God as any particular being or entity, not even as the highest being, in so far as the term contains the idea of a being among others, or as *a* Supreme Being set over against other beings.

Thus, in what has been called his mystical philosophy of the Unconditioned, Tillich grasps those insights which are common to the mystics of all religions. One is reminded of the startling and paradoxical words of Meister Eckhart in one of his sermons – one wonders what his congregation made of them – 'Love Him as He is: a not-God, a not-spirit, a not-Person, a not-image; as sheer, pure, limpid unity, alien from all duality.'

In equating God with Being itself, Tillich is compelled

82

to make a further logical step, which is expressed in a sentence in his *Systematic Theology*: 'After this has been said, nothing else can be said about God as God which is not symbolic.'

Tillich has been criticized (and the writing of other existentialists is subject to the same criticism) for his sometimes obscure and illogical use of the word 'being'; and one is bound to confess that these criticisms are, in part at least, justified. He speaks of 'being', 'being itself' or 'being-in-itself', 'the ground of being', and 'the power of being', while, in one place, he writes that what is experienced in the mythical symbol is 'the unconditioned transcendent [i.e. God], the source of both existence and meaning, which transcends both 'being-in-itself' as well as 'being-for-us'.

A. C. Garnett considers that Tillich's attempt to find a philosophical basis in the conception of God as being-itself is unsound, since the verb 'to be' has a purely logical function and refers to nothing even when used existentially.

In a footnote in the section, 'Existentialism and Theology' in his book, *Twentieth Century Religious Thought*, Professor John Macquarrie criticizes Tillich in these words:

Tillich's actual usage is not always clear. For instance, when it is said that God is 'being itself' and also the 'ground of being', the word 'being' must be employed in two different senses; for 'being itself' as an ultimate can have no ground, and the 'ground of being' must be interpreted as the 'ground of entities, or particular beings', that is to say, the 'being itself' by participation in which any entity is. Still more obscure is the expression 'power of being'. Here there is a double ambiguity. The word 'being' has the ambiguity already noted, and in addition the genitive may be either subjective or objective, that is to say, it may mean either the 'power exerted by being' or the 'power to be'. Thus the expression could bear at least four different senses, though it is doubtful if they are all intelligible. Which sense is intended by Tillich the present writer will not venture to say.

It would not be surprising if a reader of the preceding pages has not been longing to say something like what Macquarrie is saying. To one acquainted with the literature of mysticism, however, what Tillich is trying to convey is not difficult to grasp. Let us try and make this clear.

In the language of mysticism, two terms are used to cover the realities grouped by Tillich under the single term, *being*, e.g. *Becoming* and *Being*. Existence in the sense of the kind of 'being' which belongs to man in his concrete living would more exactly be called 'becoming'. In Buddhist religious philosophy, *existence*, meaning the whole of reality as we see it, including the kind of being known to man in his concrete living, acting and deciding, is called Samsara, the World or Wheel of Becoming, i.e. life as we know it, and is contrasted with Nirvana, life as it really is. For the mystics, as indeed for the scientist, the universe is not static but dynamic; it is a world of Becoming. It is, however, intimately bound up with a timeless world of Being. It is flooded throughout by the divine action and no part is more removed from the Godhead, which is Pure Being, 'being-in-itself', than any other part. 'God', said Meister Eckhart (in Sermon LXIX), 'is nearer to me than I am to myself; He is just as near to wood and stone, but they do not know it'. The same truth is expressed in the Oxyrhynchus Papyri: 'Raise the stone and there thou shalt find me. Cleave the wood and there am I'. Jacob Boehme (in *The Threefold Life of Man*) puts it this way: 'If thou conceivest a small minute circle, as small as a grain of mustard seed, yet the Heart of God is wholly and perfectly therein; and if thou art born in God, then there is in thyself (in the circle of thy life) the whole Heart of God undivided.'

There is thus an intimate relationship between Becoming and Being. Meister Eckhart sometimes used the word *Isness* (that which just *is*) which operated in both worlds. It has affinities with the Buddhist *Suchness*. Everything in time-space-phenomena, the domain of *Samsara*, has this quality of Suchness (or *Be-ness*). But Suchness is also the ultimate spiritual essence, beyond the opposites which condition human perception. We can, however, only know it within our own human condition. In Heidegger's words, 'Man is a clearing in being, the locus where being is lit up and becomes unconcealed'.

To describe one aspect of being, the divine element in man, the mystics use a number of terms, the *spark*, the *centre* or *apex of the soul*, the *ground* or *the ground of the spirit*. All have kinship with the *Atman* of the Hindu Vedanta. St John of the Cross writes: 'The centre of the soul is God, and when the soul has attained to Him according to the whole capacity of its being, and according to the force of its operation, it will have reached the last and deep centre of the soul'. Tauler employs the term *ground* and in *The Inner Way* writes: 'The great wastes to be found in this divine ground have neither image nor form nor condition, for they are neither here nor there. . . . A man who deserves to enter will surely find God here, and himself simply in God; for God never separates Himself from this ground'. While Meister Eckhart (in Sermon LVI) declared: 'While I subsisted in the ground, in the bottom, in the river of Godhead, no one asked me where I was going or what I was doing; there was no one to ask me'.

The term, 'divine ground', can also be spelt with capital letters, where it has the meaning of the Divine Ground of all existence, i.e. the Totality of God, which includes the idea of God as Pure Being as one of its aspects. Of this we shall write more fully later.

Finally, in the literature of mysticism, the verb 'to be' does not always carry a logical connotation. The use of what is called 'the mystic copula' is not uncommon. When we make a statement such as 'This animal is a bear', we are using the verb 'to be' in accordance with its normal logical use. When, however, the Hindu declares: 'Thou (the divine element in man, which is his real self) art the That (God),' the word 'art' does not imply a *logical* identity; it is a mystic copula, implying a *mystical* identity which is not an 'identity' in the logical sense.

The criticisms of Garnett and Macquarrie really miss the point. The Existential Pilgrimage is a pilgrimage which many throughout the ages have undertaken, coloured by the particular temporal and spiritual crisis of our age. Existentialism, in essence, is a sort of intellectual philosophical mysticism, using the language of mysticism. It has similarities with the intellectual mysticism of St Augustine and has also affinities, as we have seen, with the thought of other mystics. It is certainly one of the most significant movements in the religious thought of our time. It is the basis of what is coming to be called depth-theology. If one is to be critical of Tillich it is on the grounds that he is using too inadequate linguistic tools for his purpose. If his thought and writing is, however, set against the general background of mystical theology and philosophy, it is easily understandable; rarely does one fail to grasp what he is attempting to convey.

Bultmann's plea for a 'demythologizing' of the New Testament raises a somewhat different issue. Though one may not be prepared to adopt the extreme scepticism of Bultmann's attitude, one is compelled to acknowledge that there is in the New Testament story a mythical element, and that this mythical element can, unless it is understood, conceal the *kergyma* from the men of a scientific age. Our study of Jungian psychology, however, suggests that myths and symbols have a relevance and truth far greater than Bultmann will allow, and that the archetypes of the collective unconscious are centres of energy of immense power, which we neglect at our peril. Not only that, it may be that it is only through the symbols which are the manifestations of this archetypal energy that men can penetrate to those suprapersonal and suprarational depths of God, to which the great pioneers of the spiritual life have penetrated.

It would be wise, therefore, to move with caution. While we may rightly try objectively to distinguish which are the mythical and which the historical elements in the Gospel story, Bultmann's thesis cannot be accepted uncritically. It is necessary first to consider, as we shall later in this book, the significance of myth and symbol as a revelation of the truth of things.

8

The Problem of Language

IN a scientific age it is inevitable that those attitudes of mind which have become the attitudes of mind of those engaged in scientific inquiries should influence the mental attitudes of philosophers, the way they define their objectives and functions, and the way they philosophize. It is also inevitable that not only the findings of science but also the developments of philosophical thinking should have their repercussions in the field of religious thought.

It would take more space than is available to describe in detail those philosophical systems, if indeed they can be called systems, which have been labelled Logical Positivism and Logical Empiricism. Nor is it necessary for our purpose to do so. It is sufficient to say that modern philosophy has moved more and more towards regarding its function as that of analysis. The investigation of empirical facts, which philosophers have come to regard as the only facts which matter and about which anything can be intelligibly known, has been handed over to the various special sciences. That exploration of the transcendent realm, in which religion is engaged and with which much of earlier philosophy concerned itself, has been abandoned. If a transcendent realm exists, it is said, nothing can be intelligibly asserted about it; it may in fact be illusory. No longer does philosophy concern itself with or attempt to make pronouncements about God and the universe. Its task has become one of analysing and clarifying the way men talk about the world. Its main interest is in language. Hence logical empiricists are often called linguistic analysts. Their main preoccupation is with meaning. Thus the philosopher who is sympathetic to a religious view of life will no longer start by trying to prove the existence of God. Instead he will begin by asking what is meant when one asserts that God 'exists'. On the other hand, one who is antagonistic to religion will attempt to show, not that a belief in the existence of God is false, but that anything said about God is not even meaningful and, consequently, is not capable of being either true or false.

In order to give as clear an idea as possible of this new philosophical attitude let us look at it as it is found in Professor Ayer's book, *Language, Truth and Logic*. Logical Positivism originated, as a movement, with the Vienna Circle, a group of philosophers and mathematicians formed round Professor Moritz Schlick, who, in 1922, became Professor of Philosophy at the University of Vienna. For Schlick the sole criterion of the *meaningfulness* of any statement was the possibility of verifying it by sense-experience. This is the famous 'verification principle' which is the basis of Ayer's system. If a statement is incapable of being verified by sense-experience, then it must be considered to be *nonsensical*. Strictly applied, the verification principle would rule out a great many statements which it would be absurd to label as not meaningful. For instance, every statement about the past would become nonsensical, for such a statement as 'In 55 B.C. Julius Caesar landed in Britain' cannot be verified by experience. Ayer was thus obliged to accept a 'weak' verification principle, under which a statement can be said to be meaningful if it is possible for experience, that is sense-experience, to render it probable. All metaphysical and theological statements are, however, ruled out as meaningless and nonsensical. Let Ayer speak for himself:

If the man who asserts that he is seeing God is asserting that he is experiencing a particular kind of sense-content, then we do not for a moment deny that his assertion may be true. But, ordinarily, the man who says he is seeing God is saying not merely that he is experiencing a religious emotion, but also that there exists a transcendent being who is the object of this emotion; just as the man who says that he sees a yellow patch is ordinarily saying not only that his visual sense-field contains a yellow sense-content, but also that there exists a yellow object to which the sense-content belongs. And it is not irrational to be prepared to believe a man when he asserts the existence of a yellow object, and to refuse to believe him when he asserts the existence of a transcendent God. For whereas the sentence 'There exists here a yellow material thing' expresses a genuine synthetic proposition which could be empirically verified, the sentence 'There is a transcendent God' has, as we have seen, no literal significance.*

And again:

We do not deny *a priori* that the mystic is able to discover truths by his own special methods. We wait to hear what are the propositions which embody his discoveries, in order to see whether they are verified or confuted by our empirical observations. But the mystic, so far from producing propositions which are empirically verified, is unable to produce any intelligible propositions at all. And therefore we say that his intuition has not revealed to him any facts. . . . In describing his vision the mystic does not give us any information about the external world; he merely gives us indirect information about the condition of his own mind.†

In fairness it must be said that the picture of Logical Empiricism given above is a somewhat extreme one. Not all logical empiricists have adopted so extreme a position, and, indeed, Professor Ayer himself has since modified the position he took up in *Language, Truth and Logic*.

Logical empiricists of the type of Professor Ayer take the language of science, particularly the language of physics, the most precise of all the sciences, as a norm for all language. Is this, however, a defendable position? The task

* Ayer: *Language, Truth and Logic* (Gollancz).
† Ayer: op. cit.

of language is to communicate all types of experience. Is the language of science a suitable language to take as a norm for the communication of all aspects of experience? Let us consider what another prominent figure in the school of Logical Empiricism has to say.

Ludwig Wittgenstein, perhaps the dominant figure in Logical Empiricism, though not actually a member of the Vienna Circle, was closely associated with it. The greater part of his life as a teacher was, however, spent at Cambridge, where his influence was immense. His chief preoccupation was to determine the limits of meaningful language. He concluded that the only world about which meaningful language could be used was the world with which science concerned itself. This world consists of a complex of what he called 'atomic facts.' About these meaningful statements could be made. It was, however, also possible to make more complex statements which are meaningful; such statements have what he called a truth-function. But beyond this no statement could be made which was not either a tautology, i.e. a statement which provides no information about facts, or nonsense. The propositions of logic and mathematics Wittgenstein regarded as tautologies. As for the statements made by philosophers and theologians, these Wittgenstein consigned to the area of nonsense. That the questions were asked, and answers attempted, at all was due to a failure to understand the logic of language. Thus he rejected all traditional philosophizing. All that philosophy could *meaningfully* say, he asserted, was what science said. But this had nothing to do with philosophy as such. What then was the function of the philosopher? It was to act as a sort of watchdog and to demonstrate to anyone who made a metaphysical or theological statement that he had given no meaning to certain 'signs' in his propositions, and that consequently, within the logic of language, what he said was meaningless. In brief, neither philosophy nor theology has told us, nor can it tell us, anything intelligible about the world.

Wittgenstein did not, however, end there. He recognized that in the totality of human experience there was much that did not fall within the domain of science, the only domain within which it was possible to use meaningful language. When all the questions of science have been answered, other questions remain, the questions which life itself, in its fullness, poses. This realm of reality Wittgenstein called the *mystical*. To make clear what he meant he used the somewhat cryptic phrase, 'Not *how* the world is, is the mystical, but *that* it is'. This mystical world, he said, is real; we can *feel* it; in a true sense we can *know* it; but we can neither describe it nor speak about it meaningfully; it is the *inexpressible*. 'There is indeed the inexpressible', he wrote, 'this shows itself; it is the mystical'.

Let it not be thought that I am unjustifiably trying to enlist Wittgenstein among the mystics. He uses the term 'mystical' in a sense different from that in which it is used by the theologians of mystical theology. Nevertheless, one familiar with the literature of mysticism cannot but feel that, in his particular way, Wittgenstein is saying something analogous to what many of the mystics have said.

The *Tractatus Logico-Philosophicus* was published in 1922. *Philosophical Investigations*, which appeared after Wittgenstein's death in 1951, revealed that his thought had passed on to a new plane. In this book he takes up the position that one is not called upon to take one kind of language, the language which conveys factual information, as the norm by which all other kinds of language must be judged. There are many 'language games' and each has its different rules. What, therefore, is needful is to consider and criticize how each language game is and should be played. The task of stern analysis of meaningfulness still remains, but in a different form. Later logical empiricists, such as Ryle, Braithwaite and Wisdom have turned their attention to the functional analysis of language as it affects theological statements and belief.

Professor Wisdom's parable of the Invisible Gardener has become well known. I print it in the form it is given in *New Essays in Philosophical Theology*:*

Once upon a time two explorers came upon a clearing in the jungle. In the clearing were growing many flowers and many weeds. One explorer says, 'Some gardener must tend this plot.' The other disagrees, 'There is no gardener.' So they pitch their tents and set a watch. No gardener is seen. So they set up a barbed-wire fence. They electrify it. They patrol with bloodhounds. (For they remember that H. G. Wells' *The Invisible Man* could be both smelt and touched though he could not be seen.) But no shrieks suggest that some intruder has received a shock. No movements of the wire ever betray an invisible climber. The bloodhounds never give a cry. Yet still the Believer is not convinced. 'But there is a gardener, invisible, intangible, insensible to electric shocks, a gardener who has no scent and makes no sound, a gardener who comes secretly to look after the garden which he loves.' At last the Sceptic despairs, 'But what remains of your original assertion? Just how does what you call an invisible, intangible, eternally elusive gardener differ from an imaginary gardener or even from no gardener at all?'

What comment can be made on this parable? The whole of this book is implicitly a comment on it. One need make only one comment here: the wrong language game is being played.

No one would dream of calling F. H. Bradley, possibly the greatest British philosopher of recent years, a logical empiricist. Logical empiricists are essentially philosophical realists; Bradley belonged to the neo-idealist school of philosophy. Nevertheless, a recent book, describing the revolution in philosophy in our time, opens with an essay

* Edited by A. G. N. Flew and Alasdair MacIntyre (S.C.M. Press).

on Bradley, whom many logical empiricists recognize as the pioneer of their particular techniques. Bradley's philosophical thought is of particular interest. He started with the idea of an Absolute in which all reality resides; anything which falls short of the Absolute he labelled *appearance*. The Absolute, however, is beyond rational description. How then shall we attempt to know reality as against appearance? For, Bradley argued, the attempt must be made. There is an urge in man which cannot be satisfied with mere facts; he is impatient to reach out towards comprehensiveness, toward some sort of a synthesis, which will contain and unify all the facts of his experience; the intellect of man cannot find rest in anything which is fragmentary and contradictory.

The way to find the truth was, Bradley believed, through free sceptical enquiry. He therefore set out to probe into all the contradictions which are present in our thinking and experience and, as a result, arrived at the point when he concluded that, once we pass from the sphere of immediate experience to that of discursive thinking, we are in a realm of what he called *relations*. The notion of relations however, when it is examined, is found to be full of contradictions. For instance, when we examine our notions of space and time, motion and change, selfhood and personality, we immediately come up against contradictions and inconsistencies. All these, therefore, Bradley concluded, must be regarded as appearances and not reality. The same inconsistencies and contradictions arise when we come to consider the ideas with which religion deals, for religion deals with a relationship between God and man, so that, at the level of discursive thinking, man stands over against God. But God must be regarded as the All in all, in Hindu phraseology, the One without a second. Therefore the God of discursive thinking cannot be the Absolute, the Ultimate Reality.

Where does this lead? If so much must be considered to be appearance, what is reality? If the criterion of reality is that it must be free of contradiction, then we must conclude that the Absolute is *one*; any other conception of It would lead to contradiction. Behind the differences present in the realm of appearance there must, therefore, be a unity in which all the differences are harmonized. Is it possible, however, to know this unity? Bradley concluded that it was possible to apprehend it in the unbroken wholeness of immediate experience, unsullied by discursive thought. 'From such an experience of unity below relations', he wrote, 'we can rise to the idea of a superior unity above them.'

The Absolute must therefore be spiritual. This spiritual Absolute cannot, however, be personal. The notion of personality implies relations, and relations belong to the world of appearance. Personality belongs to the finite; the idea of infinite personality is a meaningless idea. The Absolute, the ultimate reality of the universe, cannot be a personal God. That does not mean, however, that It is below the level of personality; rather It is infinitely above and beyond it; It is 'supra-personal'.

'Our orthodox theology on the one side and our commonplace materialism on the other side', Bradley once wrote, 'vanish like ghosts before the daylight of free sceptical inquiry.' By the method of free sceptical inquiry he arrived at a position not dissimilar to that which, centuries earlier, Nicholas of Cusa had reached, and his picture of reality is one which many of the great mystics reached by a different road.

What, however has it to do with Logical Empiricism? Bradley is regarded by at least some logical empiricists as the pioneer of Logical Empiricism. What, however, they took over from him was his *method*, a method of sceptical inquiry; the basic elements of his philosophy they rejected. Bradley held a very high conception of the function of metaphysics. It was the function of metaphysics, he believed, to search for ultimate truth. Logical empiricists have dismissed metaphysics as a useless quest and have consigned all metaphysical statements to the realm of the nonsensical. They have also almost unanimously rejected Bradley's monism, i.e. his thesis that reality is an indivisible whole.

To the majority the names of Bradley, Wittgenstein and Carnap, of Ayer and Ryle, may be unfamiliar. If asked what logical empiricism is, they may not be able to give a clear answer. Nevertheless this spirit of sceptical inquiry and this concern with the meaning of language are in the spirit of the thought of twentieth-century man. It is the way many think. It is something to be reckoned with.

While one may not be prepared to accept the language of science as a norm for all language, in setting themselves the task of objectively and sceptically examining the limits and function of language, logical empiricists have done an essential work. If one labels them the scavenger beetles of our time one is not using the words in an uncomplimentary sense.

The logical empiricists' search for clarity has, however, undoubtedly resulted in too much shirking of fundamental issues. There has been a *trahison des clercs*. The world with which science deals does not embrace the whole of life and experience, as the greatest of modern scientists have themselves affirmed. Nor is the language of science a sufficiently flexible and all-embracing language in which to speak about the totality of human experience. It will be useful at this point to consider what certain modern scientists who have philosophized have to say.

Max Planck may be rightly regarded as the father of quantum physics. In *The Universe in the Light of Modern Physics*, he recognizes three 'worlds'. There is first the world of sense-perception; this is the world as we, as human beings, with our particular sense-perceptions see it. Secondly, though the existence of such a world cannot be proved by logical argument and, since it is independent of man, it cannot be directly apprehended, we are (and here I quote his own words), 'compelled to assume the existence of another world of reality behind the world of the senses'. Though it cannot be directly apprehended, we can, he maintained, establish contact with this real world in two ways. The first way is, though also indirectly, through the senses. We cannot, however, know to what extent the medium of our senses distorts or transforms this real world. The second way is through certain 'symbols', which are themselves derived from sense-experience. Planck does not consider the possibility of direct apprehension of the real world through mystical experience. Finally there is the world of physics, which is a deliberate creation of the human mind and changes as science progresses to new knowledge.

The stature of Albert Einstein equals that of Max Planck; his relativity theory has revolutionized modern scientific thinking. His scheme of philosophical thought has affinities with that of Max Planck, viz. a real world, a perceived world and, somewhere in between, our notions about the nature of the whole. 'Behind the tireless efforts of the investigator', he wrote, 'there lurks a stronger, more mysterious drive: it is existence and reality that one wishes to comprehend'.

It was, however, Eddington who expressed himself most clearly on the relationship between the new physics and religion. He concludes his book, *The Nature of the Physical World*, with a chapter with the title, 'Science and Mysticism'. Physical science, he argued, is abstract and therefore limited in its approach to reality. The world of the scientist, an external world, revealed through sense impressions, he called a *symbolic* world, and the kind of knowledge with which science deals he called *symbolic* knowledge. Reasoning, he suggested, was possibly only applicable to this *symbolic* world. This world is, however, only a partial aspect of reality. Other elements in our nature lead us into a world which is not one of space–time. Our knowledge of this world he called *intimate* knowledge. This world, which is not the world of science, but is found within our experience, must be given an acknowledged status. It is a world known through mystical insight. Our knowledge of it may be crude and inexact, but so, Eddington pointed out, is our knowledge of the physical world; the table of commonsense perception is very different from the table of the physicist.

If then the scientists themselves acknowledge a world within our experience, whatever the nature of that world may be, which is not the world with which science can deal, or only indirectly, if, indeed, the world of the scientist is a deliberate creation of the human mind, then it is surely illogical to make the language of science a norm for all the languages we may need to describe the totality of human experience. One cannot accept so arbitrary and unjustifiable a criterion of meaningfulness. All talk is somebody's talk in relation to some particular situation. Meaningfulness can only be defined in relation to what is being talked about.

We are thus led logically to the acceptance of the thesis which Wittgenstein put forward in *Philosophical Investigations*, e.g. that one must recognize not one but a number of 'language games', and then determine, objectively and with complete intellectual integrity, how each should be legitimately and fairly played. That means that any statement, to be regarded as meaningful, must conform to two conditions. It must be a 'true' statement in that it conforms with the accepted criterion of truthfulness within its particular 'truth'; and secondly, it must be a meaningful statement in the sense of meaningfulness within that criterion of truthfulness.

The issue is, however, a complex one, and sometimes it is not easy to give a satisfactory answer. For instance, when Jung sometimes calls the *self* the *centre of the psyche*, sometimes the *periphery*, and at other times the *whole*, is such language legitimate and meaningful within the particular language-game of psychology? Or again, when Eckhart says, 'Love Him [God] as He is: a not-God, a not-spirit, a not-Person, a not-image; as sheer, pure limpid unity, alien from all duality. And in this one let us sink down eternally from nothingness to nothingness', is he using a meaningful language within the language-game of mysticism?

Simply because all the time we stand face to face with a reality, whatever it may be, it is impossible for anyone to escape from metaphysics. Every attitude, every statement, is based on a metaphysical supposition, even such a statement as 'I couldn't care less'.

Though it may claim to have discarded metaphysics, Logical Empiricism contains within itself an implicit metaphysic, a particular world-view. John Wisdom has pointed out that the verification principle is itself a metaphysical proposition.

When that has been said, however, the challenge of Logical Empiricism has been made. Nothing can be the same again. The challenge must be met. Those who claim to make statements of 'facts', which are not 'facts' in a sense in which commonsense and science define facts, must be prepared to say where they stand and be prepared to explain what their statements mean.

Mystical states, in so far as they can be psychologically examined, must be classified as feeling-states. If they are nothing more, then Ayer is right. The claim can be made, however, that they are more than feeling-states, that they have a noëtic quality and reveal 'facts' about the nature of reality, but which are not the same sort of 'facts' which are known through commonsense perception or by the methods of science; nor are they amenable to the same sort of verification. The validity of this claim is, however, a theologico-metaphysical issue. Whether the claim is acceptable depends on the world-view of the one examining it, and on his assessment of a body of examinable evidence.

But when this has been said, clarity and precision of thought still demand that any statement made should be shown to be meaningful in its particular setting and that its character should be crystal clear.

The statements about the universe which stem from mystical experience have a particular character. They are the result of a particularly highly developed sort of awareness and are thus different from scientific, metaphysical, and even theological statements. They must be clearly seen for what they are. For the sake of clarity in discussion, I would suggest that they might be labelled *meta-mystical* statements. They are not seldom expressed in a language which is not the language of logic. Their meaningfulness, if they have any, lies in their own right.

9
The Symbols of the Inexpressible

In the preceding pages we have tried to draw a picture of the thought-patterns within which twentieth-century men are compelled to think and feel and which inevitably affect their religious attitudes and beliefs. Among the more educated these influences are directly perceived; more generally the effect of them is indirect and unconscious. Nevertheless, they are present and must be taken into account. Time and time again in our survey we have met with the same or similar concepts, the *inexpressible*, the *mystical*, the *unconditioned*, the *unknowable*, linked, in varying ways, with the idea of the *symbol*. Our next task must be, therefore, to examine the significance of myth and symbol; the term, myth,* being defined as that complex of symbols by means of which men throughout the ages have created pictures of what they have felt within their experience to be the nature of reality.

Myths, in the sense we are using the term, do not die. They assume, however, constantly changing forms. Throughout history there has been a perpetual conflict of myths, as a result of which old myths have been interfused with or replaced by new myths.

In primitive mythology no distinction is drawn between the symbol and that which it represents. With the growth of knowledge and reflection, however, the symbol becomes to a greater or lesser extent distinguished from that to which it refers and takes on more and more the character of a

---

* To avoid confusion with the common meaning of *myth*, which is defined in the *Concise Oxford Dictionary* as 'purely fictitious narrative usually involving supernatural persons, embodying popular ideas on natural phenomena, etc.', the term *mythos* is sometimes used.

purely religious symbol. Not only that, but also the idea of numerous gods, found in more primitive mythologies, gives place to the conception of one Supreme Being, who is the Creator and Ruler of the universe.

This Supreme Being is at first thought of in anthropomorphic terms. He is visualized as a superior human being, standing over against man, but still, to a greater or lesser extent, contained within time and history. Gradually the conception becomes more spiritualized and transcendent, until, in the highest types of spiritual intuition, the de-objectification and spiritualizing of Deity is complete, and all anthropomorphic images have disappeared. This transition is, however, by no means universal. It is seen happening in the East as early as the millennium before Christ, when the conception of God, and indeed of the whole universe, as Spirit, and of man as, in his essential nature, one with Everlasting Spirit, emerged.

The de-objectification and spiritualizing of Deity is found especially in the mystical theology of all religions. In the higher stages of mystical experience even the symbols disappear and there remains only an imageless awareness. Describing the 'simple' inward gazing in the fruition of love of the highest degree of the interior life, the fourteenth-century mystic, the Blessed John Ruysbroeck, writes:

Here he meets God without intermediary. And from out the Divine Unity there shines into him a simple* light; and this light shows him Darkness and Nakedness and Nothingness. In the Darkness, he is enwrapped and falls into somewhat which is no wise, even as one who has lost his way. In the Nakedness, he loses the perception and discernment of all things, and is transfigured and penetrated by a simple light.

The number of spiritually mature persons is, however, a minority, and, both in the East and in the West, higher and

* i.e. free from all images, concepts and multiplicity.

lower types of religion have continued to exist side by side. An anthropomorphic or semi-anthropomorphic idea of God still remains the most common one even today.

With the development of modern science a new mythology arose, in which the objects of mythical and religious intuition gave place to objects of empirical experience, conceived as distinct from the rational perceiving subject confronting them. The symbol-creating element could not, however, be eliminated in science any more than it can in religion. Out of the new scientific mythology came a new symbolism, which took the form of equations and formulae, which express that which the scientist gets from his readings of indications of spectroscopes and micrometers, and of concepts, such as energy, quantum, ether, etc.

The development of science resulted in a conflict of myths. An autonomous science and an autonomous religion faced each other. There was an inevitable clash between religious 'myth' and scientific 'myth'.

This clash was primarily due to the failure of both religion and science to appreciate the limitations of their particular symbols. This is now changing. For half a century a process of 'de-objectification' has taken place in the scientific domain. The scientist no longer claims that the world of scientific experience is more than a symbol-creation, a particular picture of reality as seen in its effects. He no longer claims that his symbols describe reality-as-it-is-in-itself. Some scientists now doubt whether the natural world in its deepest recesses is comprehensible beyond a certain point by the human mind as it is at present circumscribed, and are prepared to acknowledge the possibility of spheres of reality which cannot be examined by the techniques of science. It is fairly widely accepted that the observer is in some way a part of that which he observes, so that the scientist's picture of the universe resides in part at least in the mind of the scientist himself.

A similar process of de-objectification has gone on, albeit somewhat reluctantly, in the domain of general religious thinking. A point has now been reached when theology is being forced to realize that it must make a large-scale leap similar to that which quantum physicists were forced to make when they came to realize that mental pictures must be abandoned and that it was no longer possible to think of an atom as a miniature solar system or of an electron as an infinitely tiny billiard ball. Similarly, to express the reality of God in terms of a Supreme Being, existing in some order or realm of being 'above' or 'beyond' the world in which we live, has, it is realised, become less and less possible; it has ceased to be an effective 'model'. Some theologians have reached a position when they have been compelled to question whether all concepts, when used in reference to God, even the theistic concept itself, have not become problematical. Has even the question 'Does God *exist*?', it is asked, any longer any meaning?

If, however, it should become necessary to discard, as no longer philosophically or scientifically possible, a 'Supreme Being' type of theism, what shall take its place? Is it possible to grasp intellectually the notion of *Being* or *a Being*, which is the *Personality* of everything, which is not *personal* or *a being* in the popular sense? This is the sort of problem which theologians such as Paul Tillich are trying to solve.

Far from being a new or insoluble one, it is a problem which has long existed, and to which more than one solution has been offered. It is the sort of problem which was faced, both psychologically and philosophically, in India as long as 2,500 years ago. It has given little trouble, indeed has hardly presented itself as an issue at all, to the mystics of all ages everywhere. Its resolution has taken place within their own inner experience and been expressed in various types of what I have called *meta-mystical* statements.

For example, the eleventh-century mystic of the Greek

Orthodox Church, Symeon, the 'New Theologian', writes in this way:

My tongue lacks words, and what happens in me my spirit sees clearly, but does not explain. It sees the Invisible, that emptiness of all forms, simple throughout, not complex, and in extent infinite. For it sees no beginning, and it sees no end, and is entirely unconscious of any middle, and does not know what to call that which it sees. Something complete appears, not indeed with the thing itself, but through a kind of participation. . . . I realized suddenly that it was within me, and in the midst of my heart it shone like the heart of a spiritual sun.*

What has happened in our time is that ways of apprehending and describing the idea both of Deity and the whole nature of reality, which were limited at an earlier stage to the more spiritually or intellectually mature, have, as a result of the advance of knowledge and consequent changes in ways of thinking and apprehension, entered, to a much greater extent, into the corporate mentality. The consequence is that conceptions which were once generally acceptable are no longer so.

The stir created by the publication in the spring of 1963 of the Bishop of Woolwich's *Honest to God* revealed very clearly this shift in corporate mentality. By drawing on Paul Tillich's mystical philosophy of the Unconditioned and his concept of 'depth', the Bishop struck chords in the minds of many to whom an anthropomorphic, Supreme Being type of theology had become alien, and yet who felt within themselves a sense of the divine and numinous.

In the last chapter of *The Honest to God Debate,*† the Bishop clarified his position much more precisely than he had done in the earlier book. Here is what he says about the relation of myth and history:

* Quoted in Jung: *Symbols of Transformation* (Routledge & Kegan Paul).

† Published by the S.C.M. Press.

Myth is of profound and permanent significance in human thought: most of us will always think and theologize in pictures. The crisis of our age is simply bound up with the necessity of being forced to *distinguish* myth for what it is, so that we may be able to evaluate it aright and use it without dishonesty and inhibition. . . .

In many popular presentations of Christianity the line is taken that whereas in Hinduism and other religions there are numerous references to incarnations and virgin births, the difference in Christianity is that the incarnation and virgin birth of Jesus *really happened*. . . . But to say that 'the Incarnation' and 'the Virgin Birth' were historical events is to beg the question. That the man Jesus was born is a statement of history. That 'God sent his only-begotten Son' (which is what is meant by calling the birth at Bethlehem 'the Incarnation') is a mythological statement – *not* in the sense that it is not true, but that it represents (in the picture-language of the supernaturalist world-view) the theological *significance* of the history. . . .

Whether the virgin birth belongs wholly or only in part to this mythological framework, i.e. whether it is simply meant to indicate the *meaning* of the event or whether it *also* describes how, as an actual biological fact, it took place, can only be decided on the strength of the historical evidence. . . . What is history and what is myth is often a delicately balanced decision, and will turn on our assessment of the documents in general.

The whole of our analysis more and more forces us to the conclusion that the *only possible religion for twentieth-century man is a mystical religion and that all theological language must be recognized as a language of symbols.*

If this prognostication is correct, it is important that the nature and significance of symbol and what is here meant by the mystical should be clearly grasped. What is meant by the mystical has already begun to emerge in the course of this book; it will be further discussed in the next chapter.

Let us as our next step expand what has already been written about symbol.

And first, have symbols any *objective* reference? Some have taken a negative view and concluded that they are entirely *subjective*, i.e. that religious symbols do not refer to a world of 'objects', but only to the subjective experience of a religious individual or group. The selection of symbols is seen as the result of particular psychological or sociological situations; they have no other reality.

Now the presence of the God-image in the soul of man, whatever its origin, is *an experienced fact*. It is, as Jung has pointed out, thrown up by a spontaneous act of creation, and is therefore a living and potent figure. It is *real*; it exists in its own right. Therefore, it confronts its ostensible creator autonomously. This confrontation cannot be avoided except at the cost of lapsing into a state of inauthentic existence. The only way it can be rationally and objectively examined, however, is psychologically, when it must be described as a *psychic image*, a complex of archetypal ideas, often of immense power, which grips and convinces. It is encountered as the Numinous, the Holy, the Divine. This Numinous Rudolf Otto (in *The Idea of the Holy**) calls the *Mysterium tremendum fascinans*; *tremendum*, because it has the elements of awfulness and urgency, *mysterium* both because it is felt as transcendent, as the 'wholly other', and *fascinans* because it fascinates and attracts.

The Numinous, however, is also at the same time, encountered as immanent, as within oneself. For instance, the Sufi poet, Fazil, addresses this *Mysterium tremendum fascinans* in these words:

> Played by Thy Hand, the soul makes melody.
> How art Thou in, and yet without the soul?
> With Thee, my flame, I burn, without Thee die;
> How farest Thou without me, O my Whole?

* Published by O.U.P. and Penguin Books.

One of the couplets of the sixteenth-century Christian poet, Angelus Silesius, runs as follows:

> God in me, God without! Beyond compare!
> A Being wholly here and wholly there!

Less directly and more subtly, the Blessed John Ruysbroeck writes: 'God in the depths of us receives God who comes to us; it is God contemplating God'. Note the polar character of the words used; 'in and yet without', 'wholly here and wholly there', 'God in the depths and God who comes'. This is not the language of logic; it is the polar language of religious and psychological experience, a language of complementarity, forced by the nature of the experience to be paradoxical. For the God-image is both the image of something transcendent, 'wholly other', and, at the same time, of something immanent, 'closer than breathing, nearer than hands and feet'.

Jung attributed the particular form symbols take to the operation of the archetypes of the collective unconscious. What is an archetype? It is, like the concept of the electron, a concept for a centre of energy, which cannot be observed in itself but can be only known by its effects. The archetypes of the collective unconscious are known only through the symbols which are the manifestation of their creative energy.

The religious symbol when examined is seen to have an ambivalent quality. It is an indefinite expression which conveys different meanings to different people. People react to religious symbols in different ways, according to their particular mental and psychological make-ups. The symbols point to something beyond themselves which is not intellectually definable, and therefore cannot be fully rationally known or described. They make perceptible what is invisible, ideal and transcendent, giving it a sort of objectivity, and so allowing it to be better apprehended.

Further, the power of the symbol is innate. It arises from necessity, owing to its own inherent creative power. A symbol cannot be invented; one may invent a sign, but not a symbol. Whatever it be that causes the creation, a symbol can only be created or create itself. When the inner power of a particular symbol is lost – and that is possible – it inevitably dissolves.

Finally, the innate power of archetypal symbols gives them a redemptive and transforming quality. How does this happen?

The most significant fact about archetypal religious symbols is their universality. They are not peculiar to one religion. They have sprung up in different parts of the world independently of each other and have always assumed similar forms. They can be gathered together under the general title of the myth of the *divine-human* hero, of the god who dies and rises again.* Though there are a good many variations in detail, all follow the same general pattern. The hero's mother is commonly a virgin, his father a divine king or a god. The circumstances of his birth are unusual. In some versions of the myth, attempts are made to kill him and for safety he has to be taken into a distant country, where he spends his youth and early manhood. Eventually there is a return and, sometimes after a victory over the king, or it may be over a giant, a dragon or a wild beast, he himself becomes king. Or there is the story of a dark journey, which the hero-god is called upon to make, or a descent into the waters where the fight with the dragon takes place. The story of a mysterious and significant death, followed by rebirth or resurrection, is a universal or almost universal element in the myth. This death not seldom takes place on a hill, and the dying hero-god hangs on a tree, and is an offering of a god to a god.

* For fuller discussion, see Gerald Vann O.P.: *The Paradise Tree* and *The Water and the Fire*.

> I wean that I hung / on a windy tree,
> Hung there for nights full nine.
> With the spear I was wounded / and offered I was
> To Odin, myself to mine.*

Sometimes, too, the myth includes a sacred marriage with the Mother. In early Christianity this sacred marriage became associated with the Cross, which is also the Tree of Life.

> Like a bridegroom Christ went forth from his chamber, he went out with a prestige of his nuptials in the field of the world. He came to the marriage bed of the cross, and there, in mounting it, he consummated his marriage. And when he perceived the sighs of the creature, he lovingly gave himself up in place of his bride, and he joined himself to the woman for ever.†

The constant recurrence of the myth of the divine hero, of a God who sacrifices himself for the redemption and transformation of mankind, is significant. How constant it is is brought out in a passage in Arnold Toynbee's *Study of History*:‡

> The demi-god – and this is his glory – is subject, like men, to death, and behind the dying demi-god there looms the greater figure of a very god who dies for different worlds under diverse names – for a Minoan World as Zagreus, for a Sumeric World as Tammuz, for a Hittite World as Attis, for a Scandinavian World as Balder, for a Syriac World as Adonis, for a Shi'i World as Husayn, for a Christian World as Christ. Who is this God of many Epiphanies but only one Passion?

Man is created in the image of God. But God is of his nature the Inexpressible; if He were not so, He would not

---

* From the Norse *Havamol Edda*, quoted by Jung in *Symbols of Transformation*. A literal translation of 'mine' would be 'myself', which brings out the idea more clearly.

† St Augustine: *Sermo Suppositus*, quoted Jung, op. cit.

‡ Published by O.U.P.

be God. Therefore men, unless they are so spiritually mature as to be able to rest in the Imageless, are impelled by their own nature to create God in their image, to 'objectivize' Him. While it is necessary for twentieth-century man to see myth and symbol for what they are and to be able to de-objectivize them *intellectually* – otherwise they may, as Bultmann said, be a hindrance rather than a help to understanding – the objectification and personalizing of the Inexpressible is for the majority a *psychological* necessity, and the concretization of the divine hero figure is of great spiritual value. It is the canalization of the *libido*, the basic urge, into a transforming and integrating symbol. It is thus an autonomous action of archetypal energy. The archetypal religious figure, however, is never, indeed cannot be, merely a man. He must be a man, yet more than a man, a 'quasi-human figure who symbolized the ideas, forms and forces which grip and mould the soul'.*

What has been written may be summed up in a profound quotation from Nicholas Berdyaev. It will also lead on to our next stage:

Myth is a reality immeasurably greater than concept. . . . The creation of myths among peoples denotes a real spiritual life, more real indeed than that of abstract concepts and of rational thought. Myth is always concrete and expresses life better than abstract thought can do; its nature is bound up with that of symbol. . . . It brings two worlds together symbolically.†

Up 'to this point we have been confining ourselves to what can be objectively demonstrated. The presence of the God-image in the soul of man, of archetypal symbols in the psyche, are examinable facts. So far as these symbols can be rationally examined they must be regarded as *psychic* realities.

* Jung: op. cit.
† Berdyaev: *Freedom and the Spirit* (Bles).

Faith, however, equates or associates the psychic reality with a metaphysical reality, the reality of God. The psychic God-image is seen as created by and revealing an ultra-psychic reality, the immanent-transcendent Divinity. This equation must be acknowledged for what it is, viz. *a faith-equation*, the validity of which cannot be logically demonstrated.

But how could it expect to be? How can one logically demonstrate the identity of a knowable and an un-knowable? For That which we call God is the Inexpressible, and ultimately Unknowable, of whom the fifth-century Dionysius the Areopagite, at the end of *The Mystical Theology*,* wrote:

... neither does anything that is, know Him as He is; ... neither can the reason attain to Him, nor name Him, nor know Him; neither is He darkness, nor light, nor the false, nor the true; nor can any affirmation or negation be applied to Him, for though we may affirm or deny the things below Him, we can neither affirm nor deny Him, inasmuch as the all-perfect and unique Cause of all things transcends all affirmation, and the simple pre-eminence of His absolute nature is outside of every negation – free from every limitation and beyond them all.

A faith-equation which cannot be logically demonstrated may, however, be a valid and reasonable hypothesis. The act of faith is both a rational and an intuitive act, the operation of an inherent energy. It is a mode of knowing through intuitive perception, which supplements, extends and balances the rational. While it is not psychologically possible to say whether symbols create themselves or are created, it is not unreasonable to conclude on valid grounds that Spirit is an autonomous reality which manifests itself in symbols, and so to arrive at a transcendent realism, in which archetypal symbols are seen to originate in an un-

* Published by the Shrine of Wisdom Press.

conditioned yet revealing transcendent-immanent Deity, operating as a Principle of Organization, which is the source of existence and meaning and which (in the words of Paul Tillich) 'transcends both being-in-itself as well as being-for-us.'

10

The Nature of the Mystical

THE idea of the mystical has been running through this book and its nature may be becoming reasonably clear to the reader. Mysticism, mystic and mystical are, however, hazy words and have different meanings for different people. For instance, some writers on mystical theology would limit the use of the title, mystic, to those who might better and more precisely be called contemplatives. It is necessary, therefore, that what is here meant by *the mystical*, particularly what we intend to imply when we say that the only possible religion for twentieth-century man is a *mystical religion* or that thought is moving into the *realm of the mystical*, should be made crystal clear. Otherwise there will be confusion and misunderstanding.*

The so-called Mystic Way† is usually, particularly by Catholic theologians, divided into three stages: the Way of Purgation, the Way of Illumination (which is also called Proficiency and Contemplation), and the Way of Union or the Unitive Life.

Throughout man's history, everywhere, in every age, there have been those who have been capable of treading this Way to the end, men and women endowed with a wider and different range of perception and awareness than that of normal people, which has enabled them to attain union with God and to see more deeply into the world of spirit and the nature of reality.

They are the mystics in the fullest sense, the contemplatives and seers. In them that enlargement and expansion

---

* The reader may find it helpful to read the section on the Intersection of the Timeless Moment in Chapter 13, pp. 170–73, at the same time as this chapter.

† For full description see my *Mysticism*, pp. 56–7.

of consciousness, which has been the predominant element in evolution since the emergence of *Homo sapiens*, is found in a highly developed and specialized form.

While in its higher forms mystical experience is known only to the true mystic, the contemplative, in whom it can become a permanent state of illuminated consciousness, there is a mass of evidence to show that real mystical experience is not confined to them. Ordinary men and women who would make no claim to advanced spirituality and would certainly not call themselves contemplatives have known the experience of direct illumination, though of less intensity and very infrequently, perhaps only once or twice in a lifetime, through which they have gained that intimate contact with the Numinous, which is known in a more perfect and permanent form to the true contemplative.* When such an experience happens to anyone, as I know from personal experience, it carries complete conviction. Further, such experiences, when they occur, are invariably felt as something given, originating in something 'outside' oneself, and not dependent on one's own volition. They have a particular sort of objectivity and an immense reality, so that one feels that even if nothing else is real, they at least are real.

Writing of his own experiences, which are clearly recognizable as mystical in character, in *Memories, Dreams, Reflections*,† Jung stresses this quality of objectivity:

I would not have imagined [he writes] that such experience was possible. It was not the product of imagination. The visions and experiences were utterly real: there was nothing subjective about them; they all had a quality of absolute objectivity. . . . I can describe the experience only

* For numerous examples see Johnson: *The Imprisoned Splendour* and *Watcher on the Hills*; James: *The Varieties of Religious Experience*; and my own *Mysticism*, Anthology, section 1.

† Published by Routledge & Kegan Paul.

as an ecstasy of a non-temporal state in which present, past and future are one.

When we speak of a *mystical* religion or of a *movement of thought into the realm of the mystical*, we are not, however, thinking in terms of the uniquely recognizable and describable mystical experience. Even if, as has been suggested, mankind is making one of those mental and spiritual leaps which have occurred before in its history, and, as a result of a corporate enlargement and expansion of consciousness, an increase of those capable of definite mystical experience should be an element in it, there is no reason to suppose that mystical experience, as normally understood, will not be, as it always has been, confined to a minority, endowed with a special sort of spiritual sensitivity. What we are doing is to extend the restricted meaning of the term 'mystical' to include a *type of awareness and a mode of thought* which has affinities with that of the mystic and which leads to a similar outlook on the world.

There is more than one type of consciousness. We may speak of rational, or intuitive, or of mystical consciousness. In any particular person one or other type may predominate. The consciousness of some is severely rational; the intuitive and mystical are entirely absent. In others the intuitive and mystical are so dominant as virtually to supplant the rational. In some of the great scientists there has been a beautiful balance of the rational and intuitive. One finds an equally beautiful balance between the rational and the mystical in such great intellectual mystics as St Augustine and St Thomas Aquinas.

What one finds in the mystic is consciousness working at a particular level. When consciousness works thus, an inner spiritual light is communicated whereby normal cognition is enabled to apprehend something which would otherwise remain in darkness. This is true not only of the true contemplative but also of, for instance, such poets as Blake and

Wordsworth, Francis Thompson and T. S. Eliot. These *grands inspirés* are able to transmit something of their vision, it may be by teaching, or by writings in prose or verse, or through works of art or music, to others who, while not capable of receiving the primary inspiration, are sufficiently sensitive to receive it at second hand. The *mystical type of consciousness* operates at many levels. Thus, it is possible for one who is not a mystic and lays no claim to mystical experience to feel, think and apprehend *mystically* and so to interrogate and interpret the universe in the way the mystic does, that is, to have some degree of *mystical cognition*. Such a one, when he feels, thinks and apprehends in this way, we say has *moved into the realm of the mystical*. When such a one perceives the truths of religion in this way, we say that his religion is a *mystical religion*.

Let us consider those two phrases of Wittgenstein already quoted: 'Not *how* the world is, is the mystical, but *that* it is.' and 'There is the inexpressible; it *shows* itself; it is the mystical.'

Wittgenstein, when he wrote thus of the mystical, was not referring to the mystical experiences of the contemplatives, nor to those of the less spiritually endowed who, while not contemplatives, have known similar types of experience. He was concerned with a general problem of perception in relation to a particular problem of language. Yet, whether he intended it or not, he has given an illuminating description of the mystical. For he goes on to assert that, though it cannot be spoken of meaningfully, this mystical world is a *real* world; it can be *felt*, it can be *known*. It is just such a world of which the mystic is conscious, a world of the *inexpressible*, ungraspable intellectually, which yet *shows* itself, which can be *felt* and, in a true sense, *known*.

The *that* of the world! let us use rather the more illuminating word of Meister Eckhart, *Is-ness*. God *is*, the world *is*; each has the quality of *Is-ness*; each *shows* itself. What we are able to apprehend of this disclosure of Is-ness is bound up with our degree of sensitivity and range of awareness. This is true not only individually, but also corporately; for, except for those who can rise above the general mentality of their environment, the degree of awareness of the individual is linked up with the degree of corporate awareness.

The Is-ness which is of God is Unchangeable and Unconditioned, in Ruysbroeck's words, Simple Being, which is 'an Eternal Rest of God and all created things'. But the disclosure of Is-ness, whether it be of God or of the world, in time and history perpetually changes. It shows itself differently from age to age, as human consciousness evolves and moves to new levels of awareness, and as human knowledge expands. The more immediate, developed and refined consciousness becomes, the more it moves into the realm of the mystical.

The *mystical* is thus the complexion which re-lity takes on when perception and thought has moved into a particular area of awareness. It is the response to the disclosure of Is-ness of one who has attained to some degree of mystical cognition. The world reveals itself to him in a new guise; it is interrogated and interpreted differently. The mind is able to stand poised at the intersection of the rational and the non-rational.

The experience of the intersection of the rational and the non-rational, though difficult to describe, is known to many who have never undergone any uniquely recognizable mystical experience. In it rational thought and intuitive awareness coalesce to create a new form of knowing. There is an expansion of consciousness and a particular sort of intellectual illumination, which brings wider vision and deeper insight. It is not a state of bare immediate awareness, nor is it the operation of discursive thought, but contains elements of both.

There are signs that the thought and awareness of many in our age is moving in this direction. To a great extent as a result of new knowledge of the universe and of man himself, a new 'discernment situation' has been created. Is-ness discloses a new face to us, which is not the face it showed to our nineteenth-century forefathers, or, indeed, to the men of the first, twelfth or sixteenth centuries. Thus our mental and religious attitudes and convictions are altering; our world-view has changed; we see God and the universe differently.

The dogmas of religion are the translation into the terms of the intellect, or into evocative symbols, or into a combination of both, of insights which have their origin in mystical intuition. Without such insights there would be no dogma; there would be nothing to dogmatize about. Dogmatic statements, especially in so far as they are translations into intellectual concepts, are of necessity translations into the concepts of the age in which they were framed. Thus they can become out-of-date and meaningless to a later age. Theologians are now coming to acknowledge, however, that the *substance* of a dogma is not bound up with its statement in the language of a particular intellectual milieu. It is thus possible for one who has moved into the realm of the mystical to penetrate through the concepts and symbols and to apprehend the truth of the insights in which they originated and so to 'realize' both intellectually and spiritually the *substance* of the dogma. He can then joyfully say with Jung: 'My inward eye has been opened to the beauty and greatness of dogma'. It no longer presents any difficulties for him.

I can make clearer what I am with some difficulty trying to say and give a vivid picture of an increasingly common type of present day mentality by quoting from an autobiographical note which Professor Ludwig von Bertalanffy, a scientist of international repute, has written for me:

Those who know my work will be aware that I have worked both as an experimental biologist in fields like cellular and comparative metabolism, cancer research, etc.; and as a theorist in biology, philosophy and the history of science; with a touch of historical research, following orthodox critical methods. I have always laboured towards the utmost logical clarity within my reach and my work partly – in biophysics and related fields – uses mathematical methods.

Nothing in my upbringing, intellectual environment or education fostered a concern with mysticism. Quite the contrary. As a boy I was educated in the 'humanistic gymnasium' of Austria before the First World War. At the university I was a student of Professor Moritz Schlick, the well-known founder of the Vienna Circle of Logical Positivism, the absolute antithesis of mysticism; it would be difficult to find any attitude more adverse to mysticism than that of the science of the 1920s.

I dare not say whether I ever had a genuine mystical experience although I do believe to have come near to it. In my youth, and in the splendid alpine landscape of Austria, the feeling of a great union as expressed by Wordsworth and other nature mystics was well known to me. In scientifically admissible terms, I certainly had 'peak experiences', in the sense of Maslow, with self-transcendence, experience of a great unity, liberation from the ego boundary. *In moments of scientific discovery I have an intuitive insight into a grand design.* [My italics.]

I found this part of experience a complement to the rational and scientific way of thinking, such synthesis coming naturally to me and not by way of commotion or abrupt conversion. That universal mind, the Cardinal Nicholas of Cusa, appealed to me as prototype of a pioneer of science and last descendant of the medieval mystics. Cusa, Spengler and others introduced me into what I call a 'perspectivist' philosophy, for which different forms of experience mirror, as it were, different aspects of reality.

This seems to show that there is not a necessary opposition or enmity between the rational way of thinking, that finds its clearest expression in scientific, empirico-deductive thought, and intuitive experience culminating in what the mystics, in necessarily insufficient language, tried to express. Rather both have their place and may co-exist.

This 'confession' of a modern scientist illustrates what I have been trying to say and reveals very clearly this shift of consciousness in the direction of the mystical, and its alliance with the scientific, which appears to be characteristic in different ways of the mental attitude of many twentieth century men, and which inevitably conditions their religious outlook and belief.

Even if this diagnosis is correct, to state that the only possible religion for twentieth-century man is a mystical religion must not be taken as an actual prophecy. It is a hypothesis, based in part on the analysis which has been made in this book, in part on a general impression of the tendencies in current religious and scientific thought.

Nor should it be assumed that this possible move towards a mystical religion and a mystical interpretation of reality will take place in isolation, unaffected by other elements. It is not improbable that it might be allied to a religious humanism, of the sort of which Sir Julian Huxley, for instance, is a protagonist. Though anthropocentric, Huxley's humanism has a definite religious bias in its recognition of the significance of the 'sacred' or 'divine'.

It is not improbable, too, that it will contain a marked element of 'secularism', somewhat in the sense that Bonhoeffer used the term,* when he declared that modern man had opted for a 'secular' world, which, he maintained, called for a 'religionless' Christianity. It may be that modern man will have little use for conventional 'religion', and that some, at least, of the most significant and fruitful religious

* In *Letters from Prison.*

thinking will take place among those who have no formal association with organized religion.

In general we may anticipate that the religious thought-patterns of twentieth-century man will represent a new fusion of religious and scientific 'myths', mystically (in the sense we are using the term) interpreted, accompanied, particularly among the more sensitive types, by a growth in spirituality, and by a deeper sanctification of secular life, as the sacred and the profane are more and more seen as one.

If this prognostication is correct, what we shall see increasingly in the mental and spiritual thought-patterns of modern man is the recovery of an ancient wisdom, allied with and illuminated by new knowledge and insight. 'The recovery of an ancient wisdom.' This 'ancient wisdom' finds its fullest and most universal expression in the religio-philosophy of the Divine Ground of all existence.

II

The Divine Ground of all Existence

THE mystical interpretation of Reality is based on a world-view that the phenomenal world, i.e. the world as we know it, and individual consciousness, i.e. the self we know, are only partial realities. Both are the manifestation of a Divine Ground (which is the Totality of God) which contains within Itself all partial realities.

'There is nothing in the world that is not God', said the Vedanta Mandooka Upanishad. 'It is the undying, blazing Spirit, wherein lay hidden the world and all its creatures.'

'It was', wrote the Chinese Lao Tzu, 'from the Nameless that Heaven and Earth sprang. The named is but the mother that rears the ten thousand creatures, each after its kind.'

Moreover, the nature of man is such that he can not only grasp something of the Divine Ground by inference from his experience, but can also realize It more fully and completely by direct intuition, by which he is 'united' with It in such a way that the knower and the known are one. He is able to do this since his nature is not a single but a dual one. He has two selves, the phenomenal *ego*, the self of which he is primarily conscious, and which he tends to regard as his real self, and a non-phenomenal, eternal self, an inner self, a divinity within him. This indwelling divinity, which is his real and enduring self, is known by many names, the Atman, Nous, the Buddha-nature, the ground, the centre or spark of the soul. It is possible for a man, if he so desires and is prepared to make the necessary effort and sacrifice, to realize and identify himself with his real self. By so doing he will be identifying himself with and come to an intuitive knowledge of the Divine Ground. Then he will apprehend things as they really are, and not as they seem to be to his limited perception. Not only that, he will also enter into a new state of being; he will enter into 'eternal life'; he will be 'transformed', 'redeemed'; he will become an 'enlightened' one.

Though they express it in different ways according to their different theologies and philosophies, the mystics of all religions are at one in asserting the inherent divinity of man's real self. This inner deity is, however, hidden. It exists at the level of human existence as a potentiality. For it to become an actuality a 'divine birth' must take place in the soul, so that a man is raised to a higher state of consciousness. In Christianity this divine birth is thought of as the birth of the Christ, the eternal Son or Logos (Word) of God, in the centre of the soul.

How may we speak of this Divine Ground? We are faced with a difficult, and as yet unsolved, problem in semantics. Our ordinary language has evolved to describe a common-sense world of sense-experience. When it became necessary to express a view of the world as a space–time continuum, a new language, a new symbol-system, had to be invented. But the Divine Ground of all existence is not contained in a space–time continuum; It is also out of space and time and different both in kind and degree from the worlds which the languages of commonsense experience and of mathematics and science have been framed to describe. As yet no 'spiritual calculus' is available. We are, therefore, compelled to use the only language available, a language of symbol and paradox, which may be alien and incomprehensible to one not accustomed to it. The Divine Ground can be spoken of only in a language of polarity, a language of opposites, as non-personal and personal, supranatural and transnatural, other and not-other, without and within, transcendent and immanent, as Eternal Rest yet evolving activity. All these descriptions are true in their different spheres and at their different levels of significance and awareness. None, alone, expresses the complete truth. That is only found in the inexpressible coincidence of opposites which lies within the Divine Ground Itself, in that higher order which is characterized not by the multiplicity, polarity and conflict of the phenomenal world of time and space, but by a timeless, unbroken unity, where everything exists in interpenetration and mutual identity.

The Divine Ground may be realized and contemplated in three aspects; no one excludes the others; it may be contemplated in all or in any one of them.

1. It may, in the first place, be contemplated as *the God-without-form*, an ultimate Reality, which is unknowable to the intellect and indescribable in words. 'It cannot', said the Indian philosopher-mystic, Shankara, 'be defined by word or idea; as the scripture says, it is the One "before whom words recoil".' The contemplative saints of Christendom use a similar language; for instance, St Bernard: 'What is God? I can think of no better answer than, He who is'; St Augustine: 'There is in the soul no knowledge of God except the knowledge that it does not know Him'; and St John of the Cross: 'One of the greatest favours bestowed on the soul transiently in this life is to enable it to see so distinctly and to feel so profoundly that it cannot comprehend God at all.' The Buddha deliberately discouraged any speculation about God on the grounds that such speculation was both meaningless and useless. It was better, he taught, to concentrate on discovering the cause of human suffering and how it could be eliminated. In so far as the God-without-form can be spoken of or described at all, it is in negative terms. Of Him (or It) one can only say: Neti, neti (not this, not this).

Yet this God-without-form is not a distant God, unapproachable by humankind, a God with whom man can have no contact or communion. For those who are prepared and able to die utterly to self, so that they are, as it were, 'absorbed' into the Divine Ground, it is possible to come to a unitive knowledge of God, to become (in the words of the Blessed John Ruysbroeck) 'God with God'; or (as St John of the Cross puts it) for the two natures, the human and the divine, to be 'so united, what is divine so communicated to what is human, that, without undergoing any essential change, each seems to be God.' There are few, however, who are, or have been, capable of attaining to this high spiritual state of the superessential life.

The Divine Ground in this aspect cannot be called personal in any sense that we, as human beings, can conceive personality. The terms which are used of It are invariably non-personal. It is called Brahman, the Void, Nothing (in the sense of no-thing), the Dharmakaya or Primordial Buddha, the One, the ineffable, attributeless Godhead.

2. The Divine Ground may, however, also be contemplated and realized in a *personal aspect*; this aspect is found in all religions. One may call it the realization of the Divine Ground in Its activity, Its self-giving to and outpouring into the phenomenal world, Being-as-it-is-known-to-us.

The idea of God as both non-personal and personal is expressed in Christian thought in the distinction drawn between the attributeless Godhead and God, the blessed Trinity. Ruysbroeck makes this distinction very clear when (in *The Book of the Twelve Beguines*) he states that there

is a distinction and a difference according to our reason [i.e. as we can know and think about it] between God and the Godhead, between Action and Rest. The fruitful nature of the Persons of whom is the Trinity in Unity and the Unity in Trinity ever worketh in a living differentiation. But the Simple Being of God according to the nature thereof [i.e. as it is in itself] is an Eternal Rest of God and all created things.

In another place he thus writes of the Godhead:

There the Godhead is, in simple essence, without activity; Eternal Rest, Unconditioned Dark, the Nameless Being, the Superessence of all created things.

When men have tried to speak of the Godhead, they have been compelled to use a paradoxical language which can sound blasphemous to those accustomed to more conventional religious expression. Among Christian writers none have used this language of paradox more boldly than Meister Eckhart. Listen to him struggling to convey the meaning of Godhead and God:

I am the cause that God is God. God is gotten of the soul, his Godhead of himself; before creatures were, God was not God, albeit he was Godhead which he got not from the soul.

When I subsisted in the ground, in the bottom, in the river and fount of Godhead, no one asked me where I was going; there was no one to ask me.

God in the Godhead is spiritual essence, so elemental that we can say nothing about it except that it is naught. . . . God in the Trinity is the living light in its radiant splendour.

In the Hindu Vedanta the God-without-form is seen as Brahman, 'an ocean of pure consciousness', the One 'without a second', 'from whom words recoil'. Brahman as such is intellectually unknowable and without activity. He manifests Himself in his activity, however, in the 'personal' Isvara, who is further manifested in a Hindu Trinity.

In the Taoism of ancient China a distinction is drawn between *Tao* and *Teh*, which are really the same, though as development takes place they receive different names. Together they are called the *Mystery*. The *Tao Teh Ching* expresses the truth in this way:

The Tao that can be trodden is not the enduring and unchanging Tao.

The Name that can be named is not the enduring and unchanging Name.

Conceived as having no name [i.e. as the ineffable, attributeless Godhead] it is the originator of Heaven and Earth.

Conceived as having a name (Teh) [i.e. in its personal, creative aspect] it is the Mother of all things.

In Mahayana Buddhism the three aspects of the Divine Ground are expressed in the Trikaya, a sort of Trinity, but different from the Trinity of Christianity and Hinduism, since it covers all three aspects. It is known as the 'Three Bodies' of the Buddha. The first is the absolute Dharmaka-ya, the Primordial or Eternal Buddha, which is also called Mind or the Clear Light of the Void, and corresponds to the Godhead of Christianity and the Brahman of the Hindu Vedanta. The second is the Sambhogakaya, the Body of Bliss or Glory, corresponding, at least approximately, to the Hindu Isvara or the personal God of Judaism, Christianity and Islam. The third is the Nirmanakaya, the Body of Manifestation or Transformation, the historical Buddha, who is the Eternal Buddha in his bodily manifestation.

3. 'The Eternal Buddha in his bodily manifestation'. We have reached the third aspect in which the Divine Ground may be contemplated, that of *Its Incarnation in a human being*, who possesses the same qualities as the Divine Ground in its second aspect and manifests them, so far as they can be manifested under the limitations of human nature, at a definite point in history. A fuller consideration of Incarnation as it is seen in Christianity can best be left to a later stage; two points may, however, be considered here.

Both in Christianity, and, though somewhat differently expressed, also in other religions Incarnation is conceived not only as something happening at a particular point in time, but also as a timeless dynamic action, which has always been, and which is repeated as a constantly renewed experience in the depth of the soul. This belief can be brought out by two quotations. The first is from a Christmas

sermon of Meister Eckhart, whom we have been quoting so
often:

> Here in time we make holiday because the eternal birth
> which God the Father bore and bears unceasingly in eternity
> is now born in time. St Augustine says this birth is always
> happening. But if it happens not in me, what does it profit
> me? What matters is that it shall happen in me.

The second is from *The Spirit of Prayer*, by the
eighteenth-century English mystic, William Law:

> Get up, therefore, and follow it [i.e. the spark of desire after
> God in the soul] as gladly as Wise Men from the East followed
> the star from Heaven that appeared to them. It will do for
> thee what the star did for them: it will lead thee to the birth
> of Jesus, not in a stable in Bethlehem in Judaea, but to the
> birth of Jesus in the dark centre of thy own fallen soul.

Secondly, while the Divine Ground of all existence is,
in Its primary aspect, absolute Stillness and Rest, this
Stillness is paradoxically alive through and through, a
tremendous Energy and Activity, pouring Itself out into
the created world and drawing that world back into Itself.
As this dynamic outflowing within the Totality of Deity
manifests itself in phenomena, it assumes an 'evolutionary'
character, and, in accordance with the trend of evolution
towards deeper and deeper 'personalization', becomes more
and more 'personalized'. This personalization of the divine
outflowing realizes its most perfect form in the complete (in
the words of the so-called Athanasian Creed) 'taking of the
manhood into God', which is manifested in Incarnation.
The dynamic flow of Deity does not, however, complete
itself in an outflowing; it converges on itself in the drawing
back of everything into the Totality. Thus a state is reached
when 'personal' and 'not-personal' merge, and cease to have
meaning, in the Pleroma, when the redemption of creation

is accomplished in the gathering together of all things into the total Christ and multiplicity returns to the unity of the One from which it sprang.

If it is asked: How may I enter into, and so realize as a fact of my own experience, the Divine Ground of all existence? the mystics speak with one voice. 'The kingdom of heaven is within you.' 'Turn yourself to your centre and all shall be yours.' 'Hide thyself in the heart of the many-petalled Lotus.' 'Look within: thou art Buddha.' 'If you desire to pass beyond the manifestation to the Reality it manifests, learns to turn your attention from the world of multiplicity, with its labelling and image-making, its logical reasoning and discursive thought, towards the centre of your soul. There you may attain to a "simple seeing" and know everything as it really is, a unity, contained in and sustained by the Divine Ground.'

Yet they will also say that this immanent Deity, this fullness of Being, which is the innermost essence of everything, is also completely transcendent, a Divine Essence which is not modified by the Becoming in which It dwells.

There is a unity of infinite transcendent Being and the sphere of finite being, which, though it may not be called a logical 'identity', is, in a real sense, an 'identification'. This identification of the divine and human is expressed in the basic statement of the Hindu Vedanta: Thou (the Atman, the real self) art the That (Brahman, the God-without-form), and in *The Crest Jewel of Wisdom* Shankara could write:

The Atman is that by which the universe is pervaded, but which nothing pervades: which causes all things to shine, but which all things cannot make to shine.

Meister Eckhart expresses the oneness of the transcendent and immanent in his usual paradoxical way:

The more God is in all things, the more He is outside them. The more He is within, the more He is without.

Similarly, in a Mahayana Buddhist Sutra it is written:

All things in the universe are but the excellently bright and powerful Heart of Bodhi. This Heart is universally diffused and comprehends all things in itself. Pervading all things, present in every minutest hair, it includes the infinite worlds in its embrace. Enshrined in the minutest particle of dust, it turns the great wheel of the Law.

While the Christian mystic, Angela of Foligno, under the influence of this vision of unity, cried ecstatically:

The eyes of my soul were opened, and I beheld the plenitude of God, wherein I did comprehend the whole world, both here and beyond the sea, the abyss and the ocean and all things. In all these things I beheld naught save the divine power, in a manner assuredly indescribable; so that through excess of marvelling the soul cried with a loud voice, saying: 'The whole world is full of God'.

12

The Splendour of the Christ

THE growing consciousness of the vastness of time and space, revealed by the discoveries of science, could not but cause, as its implications sank deeper and deeper into the corporate mentality, a ferment in religious thought, a shaking of foundations and a shattering of images. For some the universe has become too vast and our own world too small. Everything in it, its heroisms, strivings and idealisms, have shrunk to insignificance. There is thus a sense of being annihilated, of being lost in immensity.

> The immensities of space, glittering
> With innumerable stars, moving
> Silently, coldly, each in its predestined path,
> Aeon on aeon, aeon on aeon,
> Crush me. I am afraid.
>
> There is no compassion in the stars.
>
> Time, stretching back and back,
> On and on, backwards and forwards!
> And I and you and all of us
> Imprisoned for a brief span
> In time and space, for a brief span,
> For a brief span,
> And then we are known no more.
>
> There is no compassion in time.
>
> Men are born,
> Love, beget children, make friends,
> Strive for mastery or fame,
> Or simply go on living.

To each in his turn comes the unavoidable
  ending,
Death,
The ultimate solitude which no one can share.

How, it is asked, can there be, in such a universe, a God
with whom the infinitely tiny atoms of an insignificant
planet of an equally insignificant solar system can have any
contact? How can any possibly conceivable God be one who
can, with conviction, be addressed as, 'Our Father'? It
can appear like that and, when it does, one can feel very
lonely, lost and cold.

Yet out of this shattering of images, this 'death of God',
can come, and to some has come, the Vision Splendid,
bringing enlargement and release and a joyful wonder, in
which the universe is seen no longer as cold, impersonal
and menacing, but as aflame with the love of God. And that
vision, far from being superimposed on something alien,
arises out of the very texture of the cosmos as we are now
beginning to see it.

Few in our time have glimpsed this new and possible
vision more clearly than Father Pierre Teilhard de Chardin.
In few others have the twin insights of modern science and
of the Christian Faith been so harmoniously blended. At
the end of his life he could write these words:

Throughout my life, *by means of* my life the world has
caught fire in my sight until, aflame all around me, it has
become almost luminous from within. . . . Such has been my
experience in contact with the earth – the diaphany of the
Divine at the heart of the universe on fire.

As one contemplates a universe which can appear so
cruel and menacing, the answer to one question, and to
one question only, emerges as of supreme importance.
Before it all other questions become comparatively insignificant and unimportant. Can I, this feeble denizen of

immensity, trust myself to its ebb and flow, knowing that, despite appearances, I and everything in it are safe, so that I can say with Bernard Bosanquet:

And now we are saved absolutely, we need not say from what, we are at home in the universe, and in principle and in the main, feeble and timid creatures as we are, there is nothing anywhere within the world or without it that can make us afraid.

Can men of the twentieth century, who have felt intensely the vastness of time and space and their own littleness, gain that confidence and feel in the depth of their being that underneath and upholding everything, including each one of them, are the Everlasting Arms? Can they, with Dante, conceive the That which they name God as 'the Love which moves the sun and all the stars'; or, with Father Teilhard see, luminously clear, 'the diaphany of the Divine' at the very heart of the universe? One thing prevents, the inability to see it.

Yet it is there, in the evolving totality of experience of the human race, becoming more and more luminous with the expansion of human knowledge. That is the thrilling fact, that our realization of the size and unity of the world around and within us, and of all the relationships, affinities and sympathies which bind all its elements together, far from destroying the earlier vision, enriches it and enlarges it. More and more those who can see can join in Angela of Foligno's ecstatic cry: 'The whole world is full of God.'

Yet it is possible for one who has reached this state of intellectual vision to find the idea of Incarnation difficult to grasp. Indeed, his difficulty may lie in the very enrichment and enlargement of his image of God. In his *Concluding Scientific Postscript* Kierkegaard, the philosopher of personal being and the precursor of existentialism, wrote this cryptic sentence: 'Christianity is the absurd, held fast in the passion of the infinite'. When one is aware that Kierkegaard was reacting violently against what he called the professor-scientific type of Christianity, which was current in his time, and that by the 'absurd' he meant 'that which cannot be reduced to any sort of rule', though one may regard the term 'absurd' as neither apt nor illuminating, one can understand what he meant. Centuries earlier Nicholas of Cusa had said very much the same thing better:

He [Christ] cannot be apprehended within the context of this world. Here we are led by reason, opinion or doctrine from the better known to the lesser known by symbols; whereas He is grasped only when movement ceases and faith takes its place.

Yet that state of spiritual intuition, which we name faith, is impossible if faith seems to conflict with reason and possibility. One cannot believe, without intolerable mental strain, what one feels to be impossible or unreasonable.

Let us be quite frank. There has always been a fundamental difficulty in the idea of Incarnation as it has been given form in Christian theology. The generally accepted Christian God-image cannot become man without contradictions. For how can a God, thought of as an omnipotent and omniscient Creator of the universe, standing over against man, become incarnate without what seems to be an almost incredible *kenosis* (emptying) of Himself, so as to reduce His Totality to the infinitesimal human level?

Is it possible to find a new approach through which the contradictions may be resolved and, at the same time, the great spiritual insights enshrined in the Creeds of Christendom be grasped more clearly and vividly in all the splendour of their beauty and truth?

Much of the ground has already been covered by what has already been written in the previous pages of this book. Our task now is to try to grasp what the primal Christian vision was, to examine how and why the Christian Creeds came to take the form they did, and so to understand what was in the minds of the theologians of the early Church and what they were striving, with the means at their disposal, to express.

Christianity originated in the experience of Jesus by the first Christians. The experience was such that it compelled them to assert that the man whom they had known in Galilee and Judaea was a man, yet more than a man; that he was the divine Son of God. They maintained with complete conviction that the Jesus who had died on a cross was, however the fact may be interpreted, risen; that He was still alive. Though He had returned to the eternal world, His Spirit was still with them.

That was the Faith which, in the course of three hundred years, conquered the mighty empire of Rome. Yet how must it have appeared to those to whom the first apostles preached? The idea of a God–man, who died on a criminal's cross, was 'to the Jews a stumbling block, to the Greeks foolishness'.

What was in the minds of these early Christians when they maintained that Jesus was both God and man? It is not what they said which is the difficulty; we know what they said; the documents are legion. But what did they mean by what they said? The pattern of their thinking, still more the pattern of their feeling, are those of an era from which we are far removed. Between us and them are nearly two thousand years, during which human thought has not stood still.

Whatever it meant, there was at first no urge to intellectualize it. The truth which Christians found in Christ was not an intellectual proposition, but an existential experience so vivid and overwhelming that they were quite literally transformed. Their one compelling desire was to announce the Good News and to share their experience with any who would listen to them.

Further, the experience of Christ, as it is described in the

New Testament, is not one experience, but two. There is first the experience of the earthly Jesus, who walked and talked with his friends and who died on Golgotha and rose again. There is also the experience of the Spirit of the risen Christ, an experience of a divine indwelling, of God immanent in man.

And the important thing is that the two experiences are regarded as interrelated. When St Paul uses such phrases as, 'Your life is hid with Christ in God', or, 'I live, yet not I, but Christ liveth in me', he is using a language not dissimilar to that which was being spoken in India. But this indwelling spirit of Christ is indissolubly linked up with the man who died on a cross on a desolate hill.

While it is dangerous to isolate or overstress the historical element in Christianity, since to do so can result in a failure to grasp the timeless significance of the Christ, it is equally dangerous to neglect or discard it. For it is an essential part of the revelation.

We have already pointed out how incredible the Christian proclamation must have seemed to many to whom it was proclaimed. How was it possible to reconcile it with the Jewish type of monotheism ? How could it be made to fit in with the Greek idea of God as the utterly One and Perfect, completely remote from a world of multiplicity and imperfection? Neither orthodox Judaism nor Greek religiophilosophy contained the possibility of an Incarnation of the Divine Being.

Yet the question: 'If you say that Jesus was the Son of God, what do you mean?' was bound to be asked. If there were to be any communication, it could only be through words, concepts and images which were convincing and meaningful within the presuppositions and thought-patterns of men of the first century A.D.

An attempt to place the life and death of Jesus in the setting of Jewish belief, as seen in the Old Testament, was made in the Epistle to the Hebrews, which is included in the Canon of the New Testament. How strange, almost incomprehensible, much of it sounds to modern ears.

It fell to St Paul to build the bridge between the Jewish world into which Christianity was born and the much wider world into which it spread. So much seemed to meet and integrate in that profound spiritual genius: his Jewish heritage; the overwhelming impact on him of two experiences, the vision of the risen Christ, which came to him on the Damascus road, and that other, which he describes in the 12th chapter of his second letter to the Church at Corinth, in which he tells how he was 'caught up to the third heaven' and 'heard unspeakable words, which it is not lawful for man to utter', an experience which has all the characteristics of a mystical experience of a high order; and the influence of that fusion of Jewish, Greek and Oriental religious thought which was taking place in the Eastern Mediterranean world in the centuries before Christ. Would that we knew more of the thought-patterns of this age into which Christianity was born, not merely the facts but the 'feel' of it. What was the exact character of this syncretism which we know was taking place and how widespread was its impact? What weight, for instance, can we give to the theory that an expectation of the appearance of the *Anthropos* was widely prevalent in the corporate mentality of the Eastern Mediterranean world at the time of the birth of Christ?

The idea of the Anthropos, the Son of Man, or Heavenly Man, who was God's Son, has its roots in Jewish tradition and in the Egyptian Horus myth. Did the collective mentality of the age see in the remarkable figure of Jesus the primordial image of the Anthropos? The evidence is uncertain. It is not impossible that Jesus interpreted Himself in terms of the Anthropos myth; He constantly refers to Himself as the Son of Man.

What is clear, however, is that at a very early stage, e.g. in the Gospels themselves, the significance of Jesus came to be interpreted and expressed in terms of those archetypal symbols, of which we have already written. All are present, the divine Hero, with whose birth various mysterious happenings are associated; the Virgin-Mother, in whose womb the Hero is conceived; the death on a lonely hill, the resurrection and exaltation and return to the Father-God. As we have seen, these archetypal symbols are present in various forms in the myths of all religions. In the Christian myth there is, however, an essential difference. The myth has burst into history. In Jesus Christ the divine Son, whom the Father bore and bears unceasingly in eternity, is born in time. In his Incarnation, Passion and Resurrection, the inner experience, which had existed potentially in the human soul, passed from dream to actuality. The inner reality, which had been enshrined in ancient ritual and myth, was lived through in history. The perennial dream of mankind became an historical fact.

We have already noted the difficulty which Greek religio-philosophical thought found in reconciling the idea of God as the One and Perfect with the existence of a world of multiplicity and imperfection. How could, it was asked, the many originate in the One, the imperfect in the Perfect? This intellectual impasse was met in the idea of the *Logos*.

The conception of the *Logos*, the *Thought* of God, through which the universe was created and which dwelt in and enlightened every man, had its origin in that fusion of classical Greek philosophy with Oriental and Jewish ideas which has already been mentioned. If the universe is considered in its essential unity, everything in it can be seen as various forms of different ideas, which spring from one ultimate Reason. The created world is thus the embodiment of that supreme Reason; it is the expression of the Thought of God. The Logos was regarded as next only to the Supreme Itself; 'God', said the Alexandrian Jew, Philo, who was a contemporary of Jesus, 'is the most generic thing; the Logos of God is second.' The Logos was sometimes spoken of as the *Son*, or *Wisdom*, or *Word* of God; it was the connecting link and mediator between the eternal and ephemeral. In effect the Logos doctrine inserted a principle of activity within the One and Perfect Godhead and so made it possible for It to manifest Itself in the phenomenal world.

This idea of the Logos is used by the writer of the Fourth Gospel, which is dated between A.D. 80 and 100. It opens with a Prologue:

> In the beginning the Word was.
> And the Word was with God,
> And the Word was God.

> He was with God in the beginning.
> All things came to be through him,
> And without him not one came to be.

> What came to be in him was Life;
> And Life was the Light of mankind.

> And the Light is shining in the Dark;
> The Dark did not conquer it. . . .

> And the Word became flesh
> And pitched his tent among us,
> Full of grace and truth.

> We saw his glory,
> Glory such as comes
> From father to only son. . . .

God, no one has seen ever.
The Only Son, who *is* in the bosom of the
    Father,
He made Him known.*

By the identification of Christ with the Logos Jesus was
taken out of his purely Jewish setting and universalized.†
According to the second-century apologist, Justin Martyr,
'Christ was and is the Logos who dwells in every man',
and he goes on to declare that, in that they were inspired
by the Logos, Socrates and Plato as well as Moses and
Isaiah, were Christians. In subtle ways the two great
Alexandrian Fathers of the Church, Clement and Origen,
developed the same theme.

Thus, by St Paul and the author of the Fourth Gospel,
the stage was set for the great theological debate on the
nature of Christ which fills the following centuries. To study
this great debate, to ask oneself what was the profound insight for which these theologians were striving to find the
most perfect expression and why, time and time again,
formulae, the so-called heresies, some of them apparently
so attractive and reasonable, were rejected, is a fascinating
task. There is no space to tell the whole story here. We must
content ourselves with the final outcome. It is found in
the rejal statement, drawn up at a great Council of the
Church which, in 325, met at Nicaea. This statement is
further refined in the Declaration of Faith of Chalcedon,

---

* Rieu's translation in *The Four Gospels* (Penguin Books).

† Some theologians have tried to play down the influence of
Greek thought on the development of Christianity and have
sought the origin of the idea of the *Word of God* in the conception
of the *Word* as it is found in the Old Testament. There is no need
here to attempt to resolve this controversy. It is not improbable
that the two conceptions coalesced. Certainly the conventional
Jewish idea of the Messiah was transformed, universalized and
intellectualized by St Paul and by the author of the Fourth Gospel.

framed over a century later, in 451, by another Council of the Church. The Nicene credal statement runs as follows:

We believe in one God, the Father All-sovereign, maker of all things visible and invisible:

And in One Lord Jesus Christ, the Son of God, begotten of the Father, only begotten, that is the substance of the Father (i.e. *from the inmost being of the Father, inseparably one*), God of God, Light of Light, true God of true God, begotten not created, of one substance with the Father (i.e. *sharing one being with the Father, and therefore distinct in existence, though essentially one*), through whom (i.e. *the Son*) all things were made, things in heaven and things on the earth; who for us men and our salvation came down and was made flesh and became man (i.e. *taking on himself all that makes man man*), suffered and rose on the third day, ascended into the heavens, is coming to judge living and dead:

And in the Holy Spirit.*

It is not necessary for our purpose to set out the whole of the Declaration of Faith of Chalcedon; the opening phrases will be sufficient:

. . . one and the same Son, our Lord Jesus Christ, at once complete in Godhead and complete in manhood, truly God and truly man, consisting of a reasonable soul and body; of one essence with the Father as regards his Godhead, and at the same time of one essence with us as regards his manhood; like us in all respects apart from sin. . . .

It is easy to be critical of what looks like a mere battle of words – how contemptuous the eighteenth-century historian Edward Gibbon was of it – in which these theologians of the first five centuries of the Christian era engaged. The result may not have been completely satisfactory. The concepts which were used may now seem dusty. Yet it is im-

* Bettenson: *Documents of the Christian Church* (O.U.P.). This is not the Creed now known as the Nicene Creed, which was not drawn up until the Council of Constantinople in 381.

possible to overestimate the importance of what was accomplished and not to stand amazed at the way subtle pitfalls were avoided.

In order to express the truth they knew these early Christian theologians were called upon to express a relationship which implied the real immanence of God in the world, not the image of God only, but of God Himself. There was no perfect formula through which this could be done. All they could do was 'to make and remake images', to say: 'This image will not do, nor will this, but this may stand.' None was fully satisfactory, none could be more than partially adequate. But with a sublime and unfailing instinct they eventually rejected every interpretation, every 'image', which seemed to imply a mere *association* of the human and divine in Jesus, and strove continually for one which expressed a full and perfect *union* of God and man in the one person of Jesus Christ.

The Creed, as it stands, is an attempt to interpret the meaning of a particular group of historical events, with which was associated an overwhelming existential experience. It is an attempt to interpret the fact of Christ, a formulation of a Christology, in the metaphysical concepts of a particular era. Running through it are the great mythological archetypes of the Great Mother and the Divine Son, who is slain and rises again. It is possible to use different concepts to express the same truth; for the substance of a dogma is not bound up with the concepts of a particular intellectual milieu. And indeed other concepts have been used in recent times; for instance, Hegel's interpretation of Jesus Christ as the complete expression of the divine-human idea, or Schleiermacher's conception of Jesus as one who was fully 'God-conscious'. Matthews (in *The Problem of Christ in the Twentieth Century*) attempts, with some success, an interpretation in current psychological concepts; while Tillich has suggested that the concept of 'two natures' might be replaced by one of 'eternal God-man unity' or 'eternal God-manhood'.

More recently Erich Fromm has (in *The Dogma of Christ and other Essays on Religion, Psychology and Culture*) attempted to explain the development of Christian dogma during the first five centuries in terms of a socio-psychological response to the changed composition of the Christian Church and the changed conditions within the Roman Empire; while Paul van Buren (in *The Secular Meaning of the Gospel*), interpreting the experience of the first disciples as a disclosure situation, whereby through the Easter event they gained a new perspective of Jesus, involving complete commitment to a way of life, attempts to place this interpretation in a setting acceptable to a linguistic analyst.

What, however, it is important to grasp is that, while those who formulated the Creed were dealing with a particular corporate spiritual experience which they regarded as bound up with a particular group of historical events, they could not give an interpretation of that dual experience without making what was, though it was implicit rather than explicit, a general metaphysical statement on the nature of everything. Whether they realized it or not, they were in fact concerned with the whole problem of the nature of God, of the material world and of man, and of the interrelationship between them.

Their triumph was that they did indeed arrive at what was a new statement on the nature of reality. The map of thought was redrawn and extended. There was a re-ordering and reorganization of belief about the relationship of God and the created world, of spirit and matter.

St Paul had summed up the Christian Faith in one sentence, 'God was in Christ reconciling the world to Himself', and implicit, perhaps even explicit, in his thought and writings was the idea of an 'identification', or, a better term, 'co-inherence' of Christ and the whole of mankind. Later Christian thinkers expressed the Pauline vision in the formula, 'Jesus Christ, truly God and truly man'. In doing so they asserted a full and effective immanence of God in the world. They did more; they asserted the essential divinity of every man born into the world. For, woven into the texture of their thought was the conception of Christ as Representative, or Archetypal, Man, man as he, of his true nature, potentially is. Christ is the second Adam who reverses the choice of the first Adam; he is the first-born of many brothers. Through Him men may make actual their potential divinity. Through Him the whole creation is redeemed. 'Christ was made man', declared St Athanasius, in his *De Incarnatione*, 'that man might be made God.'

This idea of Christ as Representative Man appears, sometimes in startling phrases, very different from those of conventional Christianity, in the writings of the Fathers of the Church. For instance, St Leo: 'God so united Himself to us and us to Him, that the descent of God to the human level was at the same time the ascent of man to the divine level.' St Cyril of Alexandria: 'By dwelling in one the Word dwelt in all, so that the one being constituted the Son of God in power, the same dignity might pass to the whole human race.' And again, St Maximus of Turin: 'In the Saviour we are all risen, we have all been restored to life, we have all ascended into heaven. For a portion of the flesh and blood of each of us is in the man Christ.'

Eternal and essential God-man-unity; that is what these men saw and what they were determined to express, even though, with their inherited idea of God, it seemed to involve contradictions. In doing so they expressed the supreme significance of the Christian revelation. For the Incarnation of Jesus Christ was not only a diaphany of the Divine, but also a diaphany of the human.

If in Christ there is a gathering into one of things earthly and heavenly, surely such a gathering must be a gathering of everything in the world. There are some who feel that, in the light of what we now know about the world, if we are prepared to recognize an Incarnation of God in Jesus Christ, we must also be prepared to recognize other possible Incarnations, both in the past and in the future. Whatever we may conclude, however, the truth or falsity of the conclusion cannot be rationally demonstrated. Nor need it detain us here. For the sake of our argument we may aptly use Occam's razor.

Let us assume, even if only for the sake of argument, that there has been at least one complete and perfect Incarnation, that of the Divine Logos in Jesus Christ, and that this Incarnation is a culmination of history, at least up to the time it took place, containing, expanding and enriching all earlier religious insights. What sort of preparation for the coming of the Christ would we, men not of the first, or the twelfth, or the sixteenth, but of the twentieth century, expect to find? Surely we should not expect it to take place in one part of the world only, or through the religious insights of one 'chosen' people. Would not the preparation be likely to have a universal setting, taking place in varying ways in different parts of the globe? Further, should we not also expect that the meaning and scope of the revelation would not be fully clear at first, but would become more and more luminous as knowledge and vision expanded and the different parts of the world drew closer together? Let us take that as our hypothesis.

In the first half of the millennium before the birth of Christ there took place three upsurgings of the human spirit, apparently without any connexion with each other, in three different parts of the world, in India, in Palestine, and in Greece. Through them the spiritual and mental thought-patterns of mankind were reorientated and recast.

The profound Indian vision which emerged at this time

was, in its essence, a shedding of all animistic and anthropomorphic ideas of Deity and the realization, both through
inner experience and in philosophical concepts, of the
Divine Ground in its aspect of the God-without-form, as
all-pervading, timeless, universal Spirit, in which everything has its origin and continuance. God is immanent in
everything, for 'there is nothing in the world which is not
God'. He is in the butterfly and the elephant, in mountain
and forest, in sunlight and lightning flash as well as in man.
In man the divine immanence is his very self, his Greater
Self, which is one with Spirit, so that, using the mystic
copula, it is possible to say: *Tat tvam asi*; Thou art the
That. Thus the duality between the human and the divine
was abolished. Yet not fully. The deep spirituality of the
Hindu vision prevented the Hindu mind from grasping a
full co-inherence between matter and spirit, between
history and not-history, between time and timelessness. The
realization of the modified reality of the phenomenal world
and its veiling of the real world of Spirit resulted in human
history being given only a minor significance. The meaning
of existence was not to be found in the historical process,
nor were the purposes of God fulfilled in history. The goal
of creation lay outside history. This is of course in part
true; but it is incomplete as it stands. It prevents another
vision, the vision of the world as, in a real sense, *le milieu
divin*.

I would not, however, give the impression that Hinduism
is a religion of world-negation. Its religio-philosophy on the
nature of the universe and man's self is subtle and not
easy for a Westerner to understand. It may be expressed
somewhat as follows:

Enlightenment is attained only when a man comes to
realize the identity of his higher self with Brahman. Until
that state of spiritual perfection is reached, until the sense
of 'I' and 'Thou' has completely disappeared, the world is

real. Only when the sense of a personal and individual ego has completely faded out and the meaning of *Thou art the That* fully experienced does the illusory nature of the world as a self-subsistent entity become evident.

The religious insights of Palestine stand in vivid contrast to those of India. While Hindu thought stresses the immanence of God, in Hebrew thought he is the completely Other. God stands over and above the world. He is the Almighty One, the Creator and Controller of the universe. He is not to be identified with the natural process. To the Hebrew mind the material world was not a modified reality; it was real in its own right. So, too, was human history. God, though not identified with it, reveals Himself to man through the historical process; it is the working out of his plan, something in which he plays an intimate part.

Yet, though the Hebrew god, Yahveh, is regarded as standing over against man, he is not in the fullest sense transcendent, for he dwells in the realm of the historical; He is contained in time and space. At what stage transcendence intruded, it is difficult to say. Much depends on the dating of documents and an assessment of the meaning of words in the minds of those who used them. It may not have been until the period of the Babylonian captivity, when Judaism came into contact with other developed religious systems; and, even when the element of transcendence had entered and the idea of Yahveh had taken on unconditionedness, the historical element still remained

Unlike the Hindu, the Hebrew conception of God was vividly personal and anthropomorphic; He can love and hate, punish and forgive. He is a God of righteousness, from whom stems the moral law, so that to break the moral law is to sin against God and to bring His wrath upon the sinner, whether the sinner be an individual or a community.

Though there were important religious elements in Greek thought, the Greeks were not fundamentally a spiritual people; their eyes were turned outward to the material world. They were the first culture to conceive the idea of an orderly, rational universe, governed by law, a universe, moreover, which men could, by their reason, explore and comprehend. To the thinkers of Greece reason appeared to be the most divine element in man, that which distinguished him from, and put him above, the rest of creation.

These must not be regarded as more than brief generalized statements. We may sum up: to India was given the vision of the spiritual foundation of the universe and the immanence of God in it; to Palestine the vision of the significance of the material world and of the historical process; to Greece the vision of order and reason.

Each of these visions of reality can be seen as complementary, each as a fragment of the full truth, each supplementing the other. All are necessary if one is to grasp the full significance of the Christ. And it is in the Indian conception of the relationship between the divine and human that we may find the resolution of the contradictions to which attention has been drawn above.

In the Hindu Vedanta God is conceived as Everlasting Spirit, a vast Energy out of which the whole universe sprang and of which it is a manifestation; man as in his essential nature one with Everlasting Spirit, a oneness which it is the task of those who would become enlightened to realize in their own beings. Thus an Incarnation of the One does not involve the seemingly incredible emptying of the divine Totality in order that It may become incarnate at the human level.

This idea of an interrelationship of essence between the divine and human is not alien to the deepest insights of Christianity. It is found, for instance, in the mystical theology of the Blessed John Ruysbroeck. Far from God standing over against man, there is, according to him, an inherent kinship between them. 'This union', he writes, 'is within us of our naked nature and were that nature to be separated from God it would fall into pure nothingness'. It exists eternally and was a fact before man was created in time. Even in our earthly existence 'our created being abides in the Eternal Essence and is one with it in its essential existence'.

In our human state, however, the divinity is potential rather than actual; it has to be realized in each human being. The nearest approach to it is found in the unitive life of the contemplative saints. 'My Me is God, nor do I recognize any other Me except my God Himself', cried St Catherine of Genoa; and she is echoed by the Sufi mystic, Bayarid of Bistun: 'I went from God to God, until they cried from me in me: O thou I!' It can also be realized in the active life by a complete emptying of self in devotion to and service of one's fellows. 'There is no one in the world', wrote the eighteenth-century Jesuit, Pierre de Caussade, 'who cannot arrive without difficulty at the most eminent perfection by fulfilling with love obscure and common duties'.

What the early Christians saw in Jesus, implicitly if not explicitly, was a full and perfect pattern of divinity, so far as divinity could be shown forth in man. This divinity, moreover, was inherent in each one of them. For Jesus was Representative Man, Archetypal Man, Man as he might be if he could become that which in his essential nature he really is: or, as a Hindu would put it, if he could realize his Greater Self. For the Christian to 'believe on the Lord Jesus Christ' was not to assent to an intellectual proposition, but to 'put on Christ', to be 'in Christ', so that, by participation in Him, he might be 'reborn into eternity' and become a new creature, no longer himself, but transformed and divinized. When a Declaration of Faith had to be made in the form of a Creed, there was, in spite of the seeming contradictions, no other formula but *verus Deus, verus homo*, truly God and truly man.

Incarnation is thus the manifestation, the showing forth, of the Divine Ground in the flesh, of Spirit in matter. From one angle it is the complete expression of the oneness of the divine and human, a gathering into one of things earthly and heavenly, through the perfection of a divine immanence, an *ascent* of manhood into God.* It is an *upward* movement, the realization in one human person of the potentiality present in all men.

Our principle of an essential unity, apprehended through polarity, enables us, however, to see it also as a *downward* movement, as the *descent* of transcendent God into man, of Spirit into matter. When seen from this angle the words of the Nicene Creed, 'Who for us men and for our salvation came down from heaven and was incarnate', take on meaning; not, however, in a literal sense, as a coming into the world of a God from 'up there' or 'out there', but freed from any spatial implication.

Incarnation is thus a reciprocal movement of *upwards* and *downwards*, of transcendence and immanence. And the two movements are one movement. For the poles of transcendence and immanence are embraced in the eternal unity of the Primal Meaning.

Incarnation, moreover, can only take place within the evolutionary process. Thus, we who are involved in and conditioned by that evolutionary process can only grasp it intellectually as a pattern of activity, within the spatial-temporal order, of the Divine Ground, which operates as a Principle of Organization throughout the universe and which determines its pattern.

I say 'intellectually'; for there is a deeper apprehension of Christ through (in the words of Nicholas of Cusa), 'that learned ignorance by which the blessed Paul himself, raised

* cf. the phrase in the so-called Athanasian Creed, 'One, not by conversion of Godhead into flesh, but by taking manhood into God.'

higher and into a closer knowledge, perceived that the Christ with whom he was at one time acquainted, he never really knew'.

So let us consider what pattern of activity the divine Energy, a pattern which was both a full and perfect realization in one man of a divinity potential in all men and also a revelation of the divine Essence, took in Jesus Christ.

The claim that Christianity is the only 'historical' religion is not strictly true. While the Krishna, the Hindu 'Christ', of the *Bhagavad Gita* may or may not be a purely mythological figure, in Mahayana Buddhism the earthly Buddha is regarded as the manifestation in history of the absolute Primordial or Eternal Buddha.

If you have stood in a Buddhist temple and gazed up at a beautiful statue of the Buddha above the flower-decked altar, you cannot, if you are spiritually sensitive, but have been impressed by the calm serenity of the face gazing down on you. This was the teacher who taught the way of the ending of the world's sorrow and an all-embracing compassion towards every sentient being. Here before you is the Buddhist 'God-image'. And, as you gazed, there may have come before you another symbol, another God-image, the image of the Man of Sorrows who took upon Himself the world's sorrow and who showed forth the love of God on a cross on a desolate hill. Are the two images incompatible; or are they complementary; two sides of the face of the Divine Totality?

Be that as it may; the revelation of the divine nature and activity in the Incarnation of the Divine Logos in Jesus Christ was different. Let us consider what it was.

An Incarnation of Deity must take place in a particular person in a particular place at a particular point in history. If it is to be a real Incarnation and not a mere appearance or metamorphosis, it must be conditioned by the inherent conditions of time and space. As one considers the story of Jesus, its particular historical setting is seen to be of immense significance. Had the historical setting been different, the Christian revelation could not have been what it was. Had Jesus been born in India, He would have been accepted and honoured as an avatar or Buddha. Not only did the Hindu religion contain the possibility of Incarnation, but also the teaching of the Bhagavad Gita, which is dated about this time, has similarities with that of Jesus. For the Christian revelation through Incarnation to be what it was the rejection of Jesus was essential; at the centre of it there had to be the Passion and the Cross. Jesus knew this; it was necessary, he had said, that the Son of Man should suffer and give his life as a ransom for many. And the rejection meant that the historical situation in Palestine at the time should be what it was, that the rulers of the Jewish Church should be what they were, that Pilate, the disciples, the mob, even Judas Iscariot, should be what they were.

Not only that, but as one ponders the Passion of Jesus, something strange and significant in the story emerges; and its meaning seems to be bound up with that strange and significant element. Most of the actors in the tragic drama behave in the way in which they might have been expected to behave under the circumstances. The main actors, the chief authors of the tragedy, act in a way, it can be argued, in which it was right and proper for them to act, in which indeed it was their duty to act. Annas and Caiaphas were the guardians of the traditional religion. To them Jesus was a heretic, doubly dangerous in that He was not only corrupting the purity of the ancestral faith, but also might, by starting a rebellion, bring upon the nation the wrath of Rome. It was better, in their eyes, that one man should die than that church and nation should perish. Pilate was a Roman Governor of a very difficult province of the Empire; his task was to maintain order. Jesus might be innocent; but it was the lesser of the two evils to sacrifice an innocent man, if by that means the death of many, both Roman and Jew, might be avoided. If the followers of Jesus, on the evening of Good Friday, concluded that the cause to which they had given their devotion had turned out to be a delusion and a failure, and the sensible thing for them to do was to avoid useless sacrifice, was that not a natural and understandable reaction to events? The mob behaved as mobs have behaved throughout history, neither any better nor any worse. The only puzzling figure is that of Judas. The motives which prompted him have always been a source of mystery. Even if he was what he seems to be, an avaricious traitor, he fits into the picture.

The particular quality in the action of Jesus is that He deliberately accepts the full human situation as it was at a particular moment of history, and lets it work its will on Him. He submits Himself to all the evil in it. Sinless, He puts Himself beneath the sin of the world and lets it crush Him. He identifies Himself with the whole human tragedy; St Paul uses the vivid phrase: He *became sin*. And the identification had the character of a substitution, a *substitution of love*. By this acceptance, identification and substitution the situation and everyone and everything in it was changed and redeemed. Black Friday was turned into Good Friday.

Others before Jesus had glimpsed the mystery of the substitution of love. It is found in the well-known poem of the Suffering Servant described by the Unknown Prophet of the Exile, in terms of which Jesus actually thought of Himself:

> He was despised and rejected of men;
> A man of sorrows and acquainted with grief. . . .
> Surely he hath borne our griefs and carried our
> sorrows. . . .
> He was wounded for our transgressions,
> He was bruised for our iniquities;
> The chastisement of our peace was upon him;
> And by his stripes we are healed.

It is also found in the Great Renunciation of Mahayana Buddhism. This doctrine of the Great Renunciation (or Great Vow) came about as the result of a doubt in the deepest heart of Buddhist spirituality and compassion. The supreme goal of the spiritual quest was to enter into the bliss of Nirvana. But could a bliss that was not shared ever be true bliss? So arose the Great Renunciation, which only the greatest, the Bodhisattva, was capable of making, the vow not to enter into the beatitude which had been won until every sentient creature had been saved from ignorance and sorrow.*

The mystery of substituted love; I use the word, mystery, deliberately. If it is asked how and in what way it is possible for one person to substitute himself in an act of love for another and how, by a complete and absolute submission to the action of the world, the world's action can be redeemed, it is not easy to give a rational answer. It can be grasped intuitively, but not logically demonstrated. We can put aside such crude, anthropomorphic interpretations as that the 'justice of God' demanded the substitution of his Son in order that His 'wrath' against the creature He had made as he was might be appeased. Rather, the secret seems to lie in something which is embedded in the very texture of the universe, which we, who have become more and more conscious of all the affinities, sympathies and interlockings which bind all its elements together, so that every action sets up a chain of reactions which go on indefinitely, may grasp more clearly than our forefathers. Simply on account of our increased knowledge of the nature of things, we are able to sense, without much difficulty, what Francis Thompson meant when he wrote:

* For a vivid description of the Great Renunciation see *The Voice of the Silence*, a translation of fragments from *The Book of the Golden Precepts*, an ancient Tibetan Scripture.

When to the new eyes of thee
All things by immortal power,
Near and far,
Hiddenly
To each other linked are,
That Thou canst not stir a flower
Without troubling of a star. . . .

When, further, if it has become possible to accept love as the underlying principle of the universe, it is not difficult to see that when this underlying principle is manifested in a unique way, as it was in the action of the God-man, Jesus Christ, waves of spiritual energy may be generated which, like the ripples of a pebble dropped into a pond, radiate outwards in ever-increasing circles. Not only that, but also that the generator of these waves of spiritual energy may in very truth be a Saviour and Redeemer, and that, by incorporation in Him others may be set on the way to the realization of their essential divinity.

But can one accept that the principle of love is the underlying principle of the universe, so that one can trustfully submit oneself to its motion? It is here that the action of Jesus becomes a revealing of the whole nature of reality. We have seen that the Divine Ground of all existence may be realized in three aspects; and all aspects equally reveal the Divine Totality. In Jesus the Divine Ground is revealed as Love, Love in comparison with which human love is but a faint reflection, Love, moreover, manifested in and illuminated by suffering. In the light of this revelation the apparently cruel and meaningless flux of the universe, with all its tragedy and suffering, is seen as, despite all appearances to the contrary, sustained and permeated by the Divine Compassion, so that we can trust ourselves to its ebb and flow with confidence, knowing that all is well. Not only that, we can see ourselves, not as insignificant atoms, lost in and annihilated by immensity, but as each one of us essential parts of its motion towards the mysterious Pleroma, in which all will be gathered together in the total Christ, in whom all action is redeemed and vivified. Suffering, pain and evil are seen in a new light, not as tragedy but as necessary and inevitable elements in a world which is constantly evolving towards an ultimate Christification. And, as old insights are fused with and illuminated by expanding knowledge, there arises the splendid vision of the universal, cosmic Christ, the Christ who is the All-in-everything.

13

The Idea of Intersection

MY book is drawing near its end. It has been, for the most part, an attempt at objective description and analysis of the religious situation of modern man. But, as was said at the beginning, the approach is subjective, in the sense that it has been allowed to come out of my own personal experience. This has influenced not only the choice and arrangement, but also the interpretation of the material. Thus, its appeal and value to each particular reader will depend on the extent to which it strikes chords in his own personal experience.

Every man is imprisoned in the profound solitude of his own self. Yet no man is an island, all life is meeting, involvement, and commitment.

Each man stands where, by divine providence, he is. Put in another way, he is inevitably conditioned by race, environment, heredity, education and experience. The two statements can mean the same thing. He did not start with a clean slate; he was partially made before he was born. And all his life he is continually being re-formed and re-made or is continually re-making and re-forming himself. The germ, which was himself when he entered the world, with all its latent potentialities, has been in a perpetual state of evolution. Everything, institutions, social patterns, systems of thought, evolves in accordance with this same pattern. The primal germ, with its latent potentialities, is played upon by environment – and, I would say, by Spirit – and perpetually changes until it reaches its eventual consummation.

Thus the seeming solitude of the personal self is not a complete solitude. It is in an ever-present contact with that which it experiences as other than itself, with outward circumstance, with other selves, with ideas which are other than, perhaps alien and unwelcome to, its own. Some are afraid of their solitude and try to escape from it. Others resent the intrusion on it and fear the meeting, the involvement and the commitment, which cannot be avoided, but which cause conflicts and limitations, which hurt and disturb. Some are acutely conscious of 'the discord in the pact of things' in which they are involved and from which there seems to be no escape, of 'the endless war twixt truth and truth'.

That is the unavoidable human situation. It is particularly acute in our own age, when so many certainties have been lost and so many direction posts have fallen down, when an old order is dying and a new order is trying painfully to be born. How, within this situation, is it possible to reach the deepest harmony, understanding and reconciliation, not only within one's own soul, but also between conflicting concepts, religious and ideological, between conflicting interests and ideals, between individuals, social classes, national groups and races? What attitudes of mind are most conducive to an outer and inner harmony?

The Catholic existentialist, Gabriel Marcel, drew, as we have already seen, a distinction between the attitudes of *having* and *being*. The attitude of *having* is ego-centric; in it the relationship with everything and everyone is an external relationship; in it even ideas are seen as 'objects', distinct from and separated from oneself. One tries to 'dominate' these external 'objects', to get power over them and to use them. This attitude of *having* can take subtle forms. One can conceal it from oneself. For instance, a doting mother can imagine that she is inspired by love of her child when in reality she is trying to dominate and use it. Politicians and social reformers, even religious people, can deceive themselves in the same way. Over against the attitude of *having* Marcel placed that of *being*, in which the distinction between the self and its 'objects' disappears, so that they become a part of oneself; one is 'united' with them, one 'participates' in them.

As I pondered the present situation, including the situation as I saw it in myself, there emerged what I came to call the *idea of Intersection*. I first came across the word in the letter of spiritual autobiography in Simone Weil's *Waiting on God*.

Simone Weil was one of the remarkable and representative figures of our time. In this autobiographical letter she tells how, as an adolescent, though remaining within the Christian inspiration, she concluded that the problem of God was one which was insoluble for the human mind. So she decided to leave it alone. Through the profound mystical experience which she describes, she was drawn to Christ. She, however, refused to be baptized into the Catholic Church, because she felt that Christianity, while Catholic by right, was not so in fact. It was not a truly incarnated Christianity; too much was outside it. Therefore, although 'now my heart has been transported, for ever, I hope, into the Blessed Sacrament exposed on the altar', she wrote, yet 'I should betray the truth, that is the aspect of truth which I see, if I left the point where I have been since my birth, at *the intersection of Christianity and everything that is not Christian*'.

Some twenty or thirty years ago a book was published in America, with the title of *Dynamic Administration*. It was not a 'religious' book; it was concerned with the most efficient way of conducting secular affairs. When a problem involving a number of people and interests has to be solved, the author argued, there are three possible ways of doing it. The first is by those who are in a position to do so using their power to impose on the rest the solution they want. The result is that those who have been defeated are left with a sense of grievance and frustration, and a determination themselves to impose a different solution if they are given the opportunity. The second way, which has to be followed when neither side is in a position to enforce its will, is by means of compromise. No one, however, is really satisfied. The third, and most fruitful, way is by means of integration. Neither side assumes that its own solution, as it stands, is either perfect or complete. In that spirit both sides enter the discussion. And out of the discussion comes a solution which neither side could have reached on its own, but which is seen by both to be a better one. Everyone is satisfied, and what has been decided has stability and permanency; no one wants to reverse it. It is not that anyone has deliberately given away anything. Two points of view have been integrated to produce something better and more complete than either.

What is meant by intersection will be becoming clear. It is an attitude, characterized by intellectual charity and humility and an acceptance of one's limitation and comparative ignorance, which leads to a particular mode of thought and action. It is thoroughly realistic. There is no assumption that differences do not exist. How could they not when men are conditioned so differently? I should be very foolish if I thought that I, a Western European man, could possibly think and feel as a Hindu or a Buddhist, conditioned by the very different cultural and religious attitudes and idealisms of the East. I can, however, be sufficiently intellectually humble not to assume that I am necessarily right and they are wrong, that my culture possesses all the virtues and that my religion contains all the truth.

As one throws oneself open, so far as one is able, to the impact of the totality of human knowledge and experience and as one allows the idea of Intersection to permeate and control one's attitudes, the act of Intersection is seen as possible within four different spheres of thought and action.

1. THE INTERSECTION OF CHRISTIANITY AND EVERYTHING WHICH IS NOT CHRISTIAN

In her letter of spiritual autobiography Simone Weil tells how the mystical experience of 'this sudden possession of me by Christ' led her to an intense realization of the Christian Faith, but not to any sort of exclusiveness. Just the opposite; everything came to be for her Christified. 'I came to feel', she writes, 'that Plato was a mystic, that all the Iliad was bathed in a Christian light, and that Dionysius and Osiris are in a certain sense Christ himself.' Of the *Bhagavad Gita* she wrote, 'those marvellous words, words with such a Christian sound, put into the mouth of an incarnation of God'. Her vision of Christ was, as for Father Teilhard, of a total, universal Christ, a Christ who is the All-in-everything.

For 'Christianity' we may substitute other words, 'science', 'humanism', 'Hinduism', 'Buddhism', and so on. Thus we shall arrive at a description of a universal attitude of intersection, an all-embracing expression of the basic idea.

Let us consider what such an attitude would involve. In the first place it would not be the reduction of everything to an opaque greyness or the pretence that contradictions do not exist. They obviously do; they are part of the structure of things. Rather, it would accept the uniqueness of each individual and group, standing at the point where by divine providence he or it actually stands, mentally and spiritually conditioned as he or it has been by circumstance. Nor would it imply the idea of some sort of 'world religion'. Such an ideal is, at the present time, not only an impossible, but also an undesirable one. If a union of all faiths should ever come into being, it would not be a syncretism at the intellectual level, an ironing out of conflicting intellectual concepts. It would be the result of spiritual forces and circumstances and the emergence of a higher form of consciousness of which we in the twentieth century as yet know little. At the present time a 'world religion' could not be a religion in any real sense, a religion which had the power to grip the whole man and to determine and inspire his thought and action.

The movement towards Intersection is not easy to

describe in words. It has to be experienced to be understood. It involves the whole personality, which is thrown open to the influence of every spiritual and intellectual impact, so that by an inner participation in them they become part of one, no longer other but integrated.

It would thus be misleading to think of Intersection as a purely intellectual process, as an effort to reconcile conflicting concepts solely at the level of intellect. Rather a union of spiritual intuition and rational thought is brought into play, so that, though the intellect is not asleep, indeed is very active, it ceases to be the only instrument of knowing. The whole act of knowing is carried out at a higher level of perception and awareness, a level in which what before appeared as contradictories are spontaneously unified and reconciled.

One may say that both mind and spirit enter into the realm of the mystical. What stands out very clearly in the study of mystical experience in all religions is that, though it is interpreted differently theologically and metaphysically, in accordance with differing cultural and religious backgrounds, one gains the overwhelming impression that there is a raising to a higher level of consciousness and that what is described is, at the level of Primary Imagination, a vision of the same Reality.

2. THE INTERSECTION OF CONTEMPLATION AND ACTION

The second aspect of the idea of Intersection may be called *the intersection of contemplation* and action*, i.e. the uniting and harmonizing of the spiritual life and the secular life. One may call it the intersection of the prayer life and the active life, if one does not limit 'prayer' to petitionary

---

* The word is used in a less restricted sense than when it is used to describe a stage of the Mystic Way.

prayer, but rather regards it as a communion, whereby the energy of the inner life is expanded, directed and refined by the Divine Energy and comes to permeate the whole of the active life.

Prayer, in this sense, is not confined to what is normally regarded as religious exercise. It is taking place all the time, through every form of communion and participation, through the 'meditation' in which one allows oneself to be played upon by the ideas in a book one is reading, through poetry, art and music, through nature and work, through contact with other people. One can be in the deepest state of prayer in this sense when one is not deliberately 'praying' at all.

When the life of prayer is thus cultivated it leads to a state of Recollection. The best description of Recollection I know is that given by Father Thomas Merton in *No Man is an Island*:*

Recollection makes me present to myself by bringing together two aspects, or activities, of my being as if they were two lens of a telescope. One lens is the basic semblance of my spiritual being, the inward soul, the deep will, the spiritual intelligence. The other is my outward soul, the practical intelligence, the will engaged in the activities of life.

The bringing together, through the life of prayer, of the two aspects or activities of one's being is essential if one is to live that active life, which is the lot of most of us, in the most effective manner. For, Father Merton continues:

When the outward soul knows only itself, then it is absent from its true self. It does not know its own inward spirit. It never acts according to the need and measure of its own true personality, which exists where my spirit is wedded with the silent presence of the Lord's Spirit and where my deep will responds to His gravitation towards the secrecy of the Godhead.

* Published by Hollis & Carter.

How could it be otherwise? For consider the nature of human action against the immensities of space and time, of which, as a result of the expansion of knowledge, many are now so acutely conscious. Unless it can be seen and lived *sub specie aeternitatis*, as contained in something greater than itself, it is ephemeral, insignificant and meaningless, a voyage

> in a drifting boat with a slow leakage,
> The silent listening to the undeniable
> Clamour of the bell of the last annunciation.

Or, in the despairing words of the disillusioned Macbeth:

> . . . a tale,
> Told by an idiot, full of sound and fury,
> Signifying nothing.

In the 'crisis' of the late eleventh and twelfth centuries, the Christian Church, which up to then had fixed its eyes on eternity, began to come to terms with time and history and to conceive the possibility of a Christian order, in which the religious and the secular were harmoniously intertwined, within the temporal world. This was the birth of Christian humanism. This Christian humanism was essentially theocentric, centred in God. Human action was seen *sub specie aeternitatis*, contained within something greater than itself. This theocentric humanistic impetus grew in strength, coming to a full flowering in the Renaissance of the fifteenth century. Gradually, however, its character changed, until, in the Enlightenment of the eighteenth century, a humanism which had at first been theocentric had become anthropocentric. Man had become his own centre, able, it was believed, by his own efforts, to create the world of his desires. Out of the inspiration of this anthropocentric humanism came the magnificent achievements of modern science and technology; but only at a price, the price of a greater and greater imprisonment of men in their own activity and a loss of contact with the spiritual foundations of Western European culture.

'Seek ye first the Kingdom of God and all the rest shall be added'. Those are the words of Jesus, the religious world-view, the world-view of a theocentric humanism. The emphasis has changed until in our time it has become 'Seek ye first all the rest – creditable virtues, social reform, instructive chats on the radio and the latest in scientific gadgets – and some time in the twenty-first or twenty-second century the Kingdom of God will be added'.*

This shift in values from a theocentric to an anthropocentric world-view has resulted in religion being either abandoned altogether or becoming restricted to a few specific and isolated occasions, while the rest of life, including most of its vital functions, is 'profaned', that is to say *abandoned to itself*. 'When this happens it is certain that the day of dissolution is not far off and the words of Christ concerning "the abomination of desolation standing in the holy places" apply with full force, for the holy places are all the possible functions of existence, and Jerusalem and Bethlehem are here with us in this room at this moment and always'.†

And now, as the high hopes of anthropocentric humanism have faded, there is a growing scepticism in the validity of the world-view from which it sprang. Here is the dilemma of our age; and it is a real dilemma; for the achievements which have come out of the ideal and impetus of anthropocentric humanism, modern medicine and surgery, amelioration of conditions of life for the many, etc., are fine and beneficent achievements, and necessary to preserve. Nevertheless, in the process, the modern world has lost its aware-

* From the notebooks of Sebastian, the hero of Aldous Huxley's novel, *Time Must Have a Stop* (Chatto & Windus).
† Pallis: *The Active Life* (Watkins).

ness of an eternal order, and therefore cannot frame its action on it, and has become uncertain of creating an enduring order within the temporal sphere.

Is there any escape from this dilemma? There is only one way, through the discovery by a supreme effort of corporate thought and intuition of a different world-view, in which there is a new and living relationship between the temporal and eternal, between the life of action and the life of spirit, so that they are seen no longer as separate, but united one with the other.

'Prayer', said Julian of Norwich, 'oneth the soul with Cod'. It is an activity of supreme importance in the vitalizing and refining of the active life, an essential discipline.

'Prayer', wrote John Wren Lewis, 'is the discipline of the mind (*psyche*) towards sensitiveness, ritual of the body (*soma*), and their objective is to raise the whole psychophysical complex which is man as a biological creature to the level of the spirit (*pneuma*) which is achieved by participation in the everflowing life of the Creator Spirit, Love'.*

3. THE INTERSECTION OF PEOPLE

Man cannot live alone; he can only live as a member of society, which is perpetually moulding and remaking him. One part of him desires to escape from what seems to be alien and limiting into the freedom of an inviolable inner solitude; another part of him desires to break through the loneliness of his own self into the warmth of an understanding participation with other selves.

This again is the unavoidable human situation, and it can be very difficult. To live in harmony with those with whom one's environment brings one into perpetual contact, in family life, at one's work, in day-to-day living, is not always easy. Personalities, interests and ambitions clash. One can

* John Wren Lewis: *Return to the Roots* (The Modern Churchman's Union).

create a hell within oneself; it can also be created for one, as Sartre showed in his play, by other people; and from that hell there sometimes seems to be no escape.

In compact, primitive societies, as John Taylor has shown in his description of the African scene in *The Primal Vision*, there can be a sense of oneness with environment, a living, inwardly realized participation, so that each man feels himself to be integrated with other men and with society.

Western European civilization has long lost that sense of belonging to a truly integrated society. As early as the Renaissance of the fifteenth century the ideal of the communal man of the medieval era was giving place to the ideal of the individualized man. That process has accelerated during the last two centuries, and something else has been added. We now live in an age of huge impersonal groupings, highly centralized governments, huge industrial organizations and multiple stores, often conferring great material benefits, but more and more reducing people to things, to be manipulated by means of mass persuasion, slogans, promises and advertisements, by politicians to secure or retain power, and by salesmen of all sorts to create common needs. Everywhere man is faced with hugeness, in which he is a mere impersonal unit and which he cannot control.

True, men may unite to try to change the pattern of society. Societies, however, come into existence as the result of vast political, economic and social forces which can only be partially controlled and are not easily deflected. Only by understanding the nature of their society can men guard themselves against its undermining their inner freedom and integrity.

Within the impersonal whole, which moulds them, men are, however, still persons in immediate contact with other persons. Within that pattern of immediate personal relationship there is a greater freedom, not absolute, but sufficiently flexible for there to be a choice of attitudes.

Those with whom one comes in contact may be regarded either as 'thous', with whom one participates in mutual freedom and respect, or 'its', which one tries to dominate and use. Within the 'thou' relationship there can be true community, whether the community be a family or an industrial firm, within the 'it' relationship there is none.

There is no need to expound in detail the philosophy of Thou and It. It has been vividly set out by Martin Buber in *I and Thou* which had a profound influence, first on the Continent, and, when it was translated into English, in 1937, in this country. It was the result of Buber's intensive study of Jewish mystical writings and is definitely mystical in character. It has been called an expression of the 'higher' mysticism of 'real' communion with God, as distinguished from the sort of mysticism which substitutes for the real present world a world of 'illusory delights', where 'absorption' in the Divine is experienced. One may question the distinction, but the meaning is clear, and accounts for the influence of a mystical work on many who are suspicious of mysticism.

Quite apart from the influence of the book on a thinking out afresh of the true character of relationship between individuals and between the individual and society as a whole, it was also at least one factor in the emergence of what may be called *relationship theology*. Relationship theology is not only a departure from much traditional theological thinking, for instance, from the mode of thinking which was employed by the Fathers of the Church who drew up the Chalcedon Declaration of Faith, but is also a movement into the realm of the mystical. The problem of God and his relation with man is approached not metaphysically, as something to be thought out in abstract concepts, but existentially, as something experienced in relationship. Out of the inner experience of this relationship comes our knowledge of God and the nature of this knowledge dictates the terms in which it is given expression, or, if the old dogmatic formulations are still used, the significance and interpretation given to these formulations.

The spirit of relationship theology is closely allied with what may be called *pattern theology*, where again there is a shift from abstract, metaphysical to psychological and biological concepts of patterns of activity.

There has in some quarters been a tendency, however, to express relationship theology in exaggerated forms. God, it is said, is only, or primarily, to be found in the relationship between the self and other selves. To express it in that way is to sweep aside the evidence of much of the most profound spiritual experience of the human race. God, it is true, can be met in all the patterns and activities of the present life. Christ is, in Bonhoeffer's phrase, 'the Man for others'. But it is equally true, as someone said, that unless a man can find God within himself, in the depths of his own solitude, he will never find Him at all. And it may be that until one has found and been transformed by Him there, one will not be able to attain to the vision which enables one to see Him, not only in other people, but also in everything. Thus, at that level of spiritual experience the poles of solitude and community can merge and harmonize in an inner unity, no longer irreconcilable opposites, but complementary.

4. THE INTERSECTION OF THE TIMELESS MOMENT

In 'the intersection of the timeless moment', that sudden moment of intuitive mystical perception, for most rare, elusive and fleeting, yet for those who have known it deeply illuminating and transforming, Intersection finds its most profound expression. In it time intersects with timelessness, man's spirit with God's spirit.

The experience of the Intersection of the Timeless Moment is more than a movement into the realm of the mystical, as defined earlier in this book. It is truly mystical in the more limited sénse. It must, moreover, be clearly distinguished from such phenomena as clairvoyance, telepathy and extra-sensory perception, which are better termed psychic.

Mystical experience, as we have seen, can take place at several levels. In its highest form it is known only to the true contemplative, and of it at this level there are numerous descriptions in the writings of the great mystics.* But

> . . . To apprehend
> The point of intersection of the timeless
> With time, is an occupation for the saint –
> No occupation either, but something given
> And taken, in a lifetime's death in love,
> Ardour and selflessness and self surrender.†

To many, however, who are not in any sense contemplatives, how many it is impossible to say, there have, as we have already seen, come experiences which, on all the evidence, one can only conclude are in the same continuum as those of the contemplatives and fall within the same type of experience, though they are in a less intense and permanent form, and spring from the same sort of contact with the Numinous. In some scientific circles, to avoid confusion and to differentiate them from the more profound experiences of the true contemplatives, the term 'peak experience' is sometimes used.

They may be of the type which T. S. Eliot seems to be describing in the poem quoted from above:

> . . . the unattended
> Moment, the moment in and out of time,
> The distraction fit, lost in a shaft of sunlight,
> The wild thyme unseen, or the winter lightning,

---

* See the Anthology in *Mysticism.*
† T. S. Eliot: *The Dry Salvages* (Faber & Faber).

> Or the waterfall, or music heard so deeply
> That it is not heard at all, but you are the music
> While the music lasts.

Or they may be more profound, standing out in their own uniqueness from every other experience, with an immense transforming quality, so that one who has had such an experience can never be the same again. Such an experience is described by Warner Allen in his book, *The Timeless Moment*,* and caused him to exclaim:

Something has happened to me – I am utterly amazed – can this be that? (*That* being the answer to the riddle of life) – but it is too simple – I always knew it – it is remembering an old forgotten secret – like coming home – I am not 'I', not the 'I' I thought – there is no death – peace passing understanding – yet how unworthy I –

One is enabled to recognize these experiences as truly mystical in character since they invariably contain some at least of the known and recognized characteristics of mystical states. In *Mysticism* I listed seven characteristics of such states.

1. They defy expression in terms which are fully intelligible to those who have not had some analogous experience.
2. Though states of feeling they are also states of knowledge, resulting in a deeper insight into the nature of things.
3. Except in the case of true contemplatives, when they can result in a permanent shift of consciousness, they are infrequent and of short duration.
4. They convey the sense of something 'given', not dependent on one's own volition.
5. There is a consciousness of the oneness of everything.
6. They also have a sense of timelessness.
7. There is forced on one the conviction that the familiar phenomenal *ego* is not the real *I*.

* Published by Faber & Faber.

That such experiences give a sense of complete certainty is recognized. What is of more importance for our purpose is whether or not they have a reliable noëtic quality. Do they indeed, as I would argue, open up vistas of reality, which cannot be apprehended by the rational faculty, in which one can place reliance and regard as valid. On the evidence of the experiences I have described earlier in this book, I personally can have no doubt. The mystical experience of the coincidence of opposites, of which I have told, gave me the key to a truth which I have, over the years, been able to explore rationally, and which has expanded in meaning and significance. Had the experience been an isolated one, perhaps I might have doubted its noëtic quality except for myself. But the truth it contained for me I found was confirmed in the totality of the experience of mankind. As I have told, it appeared again and again in different guises, until at length it was clearly apparent in the complementarity of the quantum physicists.

As I draw near to the end of a long active life, I have come to regard a capacity for what I have called Intersection as perhaps the most essential quality of mind and spirit needed by twentieth-century man, placed as he is, in a distracted, divided world, with all its conflicting loyalties, and called upon to assimilate and reconcile within himself so many conflicting truths. Intersection is a way of harmonized and harmonizing life, demanding in a high degree moral and intellectual virtues of charity and humility, and a capacity for selfless seeing. On the Christian – so it seems to me – it is binding, if he is to live to the full the life of charity as described by St Paul in the well-known thirteenth chapter of his first letter to the Christians at Corinth. And for some Christians, who cannot escape from that exclusiveness which has so often sullied the thought of the Christian Church and caused it to commit so many crimes, it is not always easy.

How is it possible for you and me, if we wish to do so, to

attain to this state of Intersection, so that it becomes a part of us, a pattern of inner life capable of gripping thought and action? It is only by spontaneously throwing ourselves open, humbly and lovingly, to – I can think of no better word to express what I mean than Meister Eckhart's – to Is-ness in all its fullness.

Science is not enough, religion is not enough, art is not enough, politics and economics are not enough, nor is love, nor is duty, nor is action however disinterested, nor, however sublime, is contemplation. Nothing short of everything will really do.*

To try to follow the way of Intersection must be primarily an individual adventure; it is something to be sought and cultivated by those who would and can. Sometimes, however, the Idea of Intersection takes on an extended form in my mind, in the dream of a Community of the Intersection coming into existence, which would express the idea in a corporate form. It would have similarities to the Iona Community, which Dr George MacLeod founded in the Presbyterian Church of Scotland, and which has proved so successful both in its conception and the way it has worked. It would, however, be much wider in scope and intention. For it would include men and women of varying types, abilities and beliefs, not Christians only but also those of other faiths, scientists and humanists, artists, poets and musicians, and men of affairs.

How, it will immediately be asked, could such a community have any sort of homogeneity? It would not be at the intellectual level. Each member of the Community would remain at the point where he stands, and ought to stand if he is to be true to himself, as a result of his own life and experience, until such time as he is impelled to move from it. The homogeneity would evolve at a higher level, since each member of the Community would be animated by, indeed

* Aldous Huxley: *Island* (Chatto & Windus; Penguin Books).

vowed to, a deep intellectual charity, sympathy and humility. Thus, both by the very fact of its existence and also by its members gathering together in a quiet retreat, living in close contact for a time, engaging in corporate meditation and that sort of prayer, in which mind and spirit are thrown open to influences outside one's own limited perception, a particular sort of mutual mental sympathy and integration would develop. That this can happen is a known fact. How it happens or what exactly happens is difficult to describe, except to say that there come moments of intellectual illumination, with a shift of awareness and an expansion of vision, so that possibilities are seen which had not been seen before. When those who have attained this level write to each other, talk with each other or gather round a conference table, conversation and discussion are on a different plane. Ideas come together and interfuse; there is a deeper understanding. Thus, anything which might emanate from such a Community would have a different flavour and character than, for instance, a statement resulting from a group of people trying to iron out their differences. Out of such an intimate association of men, each eminent in his particular field and primarily engaged in his own specialism, might come those unifying concepts and integrated thought-patterns for which we are searching.

Such a Community might be initiated by a small group of men and women, eminent in their particular fields, who, through a long, rich life, had matured in wisdom, understanding and mental and spiritual insight. They would quickly gather round them a group of younger men to carry on the work when they had gone.

Like the Iona Community, such a Community, for its success, would need a permanent centre, a Community House, to which members of the Community could retire when they wished and in which groups of people, not members of the Community, but intent on the same quest, would come for short periods. I shall never forget the week I spent at the Abbey of Iona, with its combination of morning and evening offices, quiet meditation, lectures and discussion, swimming, dreaming and wandering.

Perhaps one day a new St Benedict will arise to found such a Community, an Order more truly catholic than anything that has yet appeared. Perhaps, more likely, it might be the work of a small group of the sort described above. Its influence could be immense. At least, it is not an impractical dream. Perhaps it is a very practical and indeed necessary one.

14

Epilogue: He who sees not God everywhere, sees Him truly nowhere

SOMETHING is happening in the world. The human race has packed up its tents and is once more on the march. Political, social and economic institutions, secular and religious thought-patterns and attitudes, are in the melting pot. The old foundations have been shaken, the old images shattered, the old models have proved inadequate. The new spiritual wine cannot be contained in the old conceptual bottles.

Our analysis of the present situation has led to the hypothesis that we are in the midst of one of those evolutionary mental and spiritual 'leaps' which have happened before in history, that what we see happening around us is an enlargement of human consciousness, a widening of perception and a natural growth in the collective soul of mankind. Is-ness discloses itself to us in ways different from those it disclosed itself to our forefathers, so that we are compelled to interrogate and interpret the universe in a way which our knowledge of the operation of mystical consciousness and insight impels us to call mystical. I have therefore called this 'disclosure' or 'discernment' situation (to use terms which some writers are now using) a movement into the realm of the mystical. In this situation we have to live, think and act. What more can be said?

We ought not to let ourselves be satisfied with the God we have thought of [said Meister Eckhart], for when the thought slips the mind, that God slips with it. What we want is the reality of God exalted far above any thought or creature.

In the literature of mysticism one finds descriptions of a state which is called a Dark Night. As souls, accustomed to rely on the dogmatic, doctrinal and historical elements of religion, become more spiritually mature, the particular symbolic structure of their religion tends to collapse, the image of God to which they have been accustomed fades, the familiar props and landmarks are left behind. As a result they feel a sense of emptiness, aridity and desolation. The consciousness of the Divine Presence, radiated through the old symbols, has disappeared.*

Without stretching the accepted meaning of the phrase too much, it may be said that at the present time the world is going through a sort of corporate Dark Night, caused by the collapse of old images and models, and also, in a somewhat different way, by the stresses arising out of the breakup, as a result of technological advance, of those old social, economic and environmental patterns which gave a sense of community and were the patterns in which religious life and practice had their secular setting.

The type of person for whom in the past religion was little more than a form of escapism or a conformity to social custom is little affected by this Dark Night. He takes refuge in the inauthentic existence of television and football pools, of motor cars and the latest 'pop' tune. For the more sensitive the Dark Night can be painful. Life can cease to have meaning; faith can be lost.

Yet the Dark Night can be a prelude to a greater spiritual maturity and lead to a new and deeper vision of God. One need not be worried, therefore, because the old images of God may have gone. God has no name, though He is called by a hundred names. He has no form, though He is manifested through a thousand forms. Only when, it has been said, a man frees his idea of God from special forms can it for him fill all forms. Every image, every name, every idea of

* The state of the Dark Night must not be confused with that known as the Divine Dark or the Cloud of Unknowing, which are quite different. (See *Mysticism*, Anthology, sections 9 and 19.)

God is a symbol, which can be a pathway into the Inexpressible, but is a symbol none the less.

The divine essence by its immensity surpasses every form
to which our intellect reaches; and thus we cannot apprehend
it by knowing what it is.

So wrote the Catholic saint, Thomas Aquinas, and he is
echoed by the Zen Buddhist, Hsuan-chiao, already quoted:

You cannot take hold of it, nor can you get rid of it;
While you can do neither, it goes on its own way;
You remain silent and it speaks; you speak and it is silent.

But if it is not possible to *think* God, how can one who is
not particularly spiritual, whose life is spent in the ordinary
activities of the world, whose outlook is that of one who is
now being called a 'secular' man, hope to grasp His reality?

'God is the most obvious thing in the world', wrote Alan
W. Watt (in *Behold the Spirit*). 'He is absolutely self-
evident – the simplest, clearest and closest reality of life and
consciousness. We are only unaware of Him because we are
too complicated, for our vision is darkened by the complexity of pride. We seek beyond the horizon with our noses
lifted high in the air, and fail to see that He lies at our very
feet. . . . We are like birds flying in quest of air, or men with
lighted candles searching through the darkness for fire'.

If the That we call God is Is-ness itself, how could it be
otherwise? 'God is as pervasive and perceptible', wrote
Father Teilhard in *Le Milieu Divin*, 'as the atmosphere in
which we are bathed. He encompasses us on all sides, like
the world itself. What prevents you, then, from enfolding
Him in your arms?' And he gives the answer: 'Only one
thing; your inability *to see Him*'.

There is the rub; our inability to see the obvious. Somehow the obvious thing is for many difficult to see. What is
to be done about it? How can twentieth-century secular man,
who seems to have lost God, find again for himself the

reality of God? How can one for whom life has ceased to have meaning once more learn to see everything as a diaphany of the divine indwelling?

There are some who are capable of scaling the dizzy spiritual heights, but that adventure is for the few. For the majority there is another way, which is the way proper for them.

When, in the Bhagavad Gita, Prince Arjuna asked Krishna to tell him one definite way of reaching the highest good, Krishna replied that there was not one way but two, for the contemplative the path of spiritual knowledge, for the active man the path of dedicated action:

Now you shall hear how a man may become perfect, by devoting himself to the work which is natural to him. A man will reach perfection if he does his work as an act of worship to the Lord, who is the source of the universe, prompting all action, everywhere present.

God can be found far beyond the polar circle of the mind; He can be equally found in the intimacy of the present Now. The present moment is for most of us the focal point of reality, 'the elusive image of eternity, so small that it has no temporal length and yet so long that we can never escape from it'.

If that be so, if for us God may be realized, i.e. become real, in the here and now, then that is the place in which to look for him, in the very texture of all our living, in our work, in the people with whom we come in contact, in the things around us. And not in our active life only, but also within our own souls; for it is there the kingdom of heaven has its seat. Everywhere; always; there, when our eyes are opened, God can become intensely real. 'He who sees not God everywhere', wrote a master of the spiritual life, 'sees Him truly nowhere'.

There is a delightful story told of a Zen Buddhist novice who asked the master of the monastery for some spiritual instruction. 'You have had your breakfast?' asked the master. 'Yes', answered the novice. 'Then', said the master, 'go and wash the dishes'.

It all sounds very simple, too simple to be true. Yet when, in interior recollection, selflessness and desire – and the desire is everything – men have.followed the path of what is for them the equivalent of washing the dishes, they have in the end found the hidden treasure.

Index

This book does not lend itself to indexing except in an impossibly elaborate form. This short index of proper names and of works mentioned, and in some cases quoted from, will help the reader to find some topic to which he may want to refer. The references to Christ, Christianity and the Christian Church are so numerous that to index them appeared to be neither necessary nor possible.